MASTERCHEF
1995

MASTERCHEF 1995

FOREWORD BY LOYD GROSSMAN

GENERAL EDITOR: JANET ILLSLEY

VERMILION
LONDON

First published 1995

Compilation copyright © Union Pictures 1995
Recipes copyright © The Contributors 1995
Foreword © Loyd Grossman 1995
Introduction © Richard Bryan 1995
Photographs © Ebury Press 1995
Front Cover Photograph © Ebury Press 1995
Back cover photograph © Richard Farley 1995

First published in the United Kingdom in 1995 by Vermilion, an imprint of Ebury Press, Random House, 20 Vauxhall Bridge Road, London SW1V 2SA

Random House Australia (Pty) Limited
20 Alfred Street, Milsons Point, Sydney,
New South Wales 2061, Australia

Random House New Zealand Limited
18 Poland Road, Glenfield
Auckland 10, New Zealand

Random House South Africa (Pty) Limited
PO BOX 337, Bergvlei, South Africa

Random House UK Limited Reg. No. 954009

A CIP catalogue record for this book is available from the British Library

ISBN: 0 09 180683 6

MasterChef 1995
A Union Pictures production for BBC North
Series devised by Franc Roddam
Executive Producers: Bradley Adams and Richard Kalms
Producer and Director: Richard Bryan
Associate Producer: Glynis Robertson
Production Co-ordinators: Melanie Jappy, Julie Dixon and Julia Park

General Editor: Janet Illsley
Design: Clive Dorman
Front cover photograph: Ken Field
Inside photographs: Gus Filgate
Food Stylist: Louise Pickford
Photographic Stylist: Penny Markham

Typeset by Clive Dorman & Co.
Printed and bound in Great Britain by Mackays of Chatham plc, Kent

Papers used by Ebury Press are natural recyclable products made from wood grown in sustainable forests.

CONTENTS

FOREWORD

The actual recording of MasterChef is an extraordinary experience because suddenly all the work over so many months for our contestants, our judges from around the country, and our production team comes together for a very intense fortnight of filming. Our television studio is miraculously transformed from an empty though rather high-tech shed, thanks to the installation of our, by now, celebrated red, yellow and blue kitchens, our splendid video wall, our sofa and chairs, and an effigy – supposedly of me – which has graced our stage for the last two series! Last year 'The Thing' wore a green suit of military hue which led it to be nicknamed 'Sergeant Bilko'. This year Bilko was repainted in designer tartan, no new nickname emerged and I am hoping – probably vainly – that next year it will go away quietly!

Many people ask me "Do you cook?" I am sometimes taken a little aback by this question as I think it would be difficult to be so interested in food without cooking. Whilst I endorse the feeling of many chefs that to be a good cook you must be a good eater, I must say that for me the pleasure of cooking comes just behind the pleasure of eating. "Would I cook on MasterChef?" I suppose the answer would be yes, if I were good enough and if I weren't already on the show, but fortunately for me the question is hypothetical. What isn't hypothetical is the intensely impassioned performance that all our contestants bring to the party. Sometimes they are nervous, sometimes they do make mistakes, sometimes they do things a professional chef wouldn't. And that as far as I'm concerned is all for the better because they cook with an emotion and intensity that can be lacking in many professional kitchens. They also bring a freedom to cooking and willingness to experiment that is a joy to behold, and a thrill to eat.

In the early days of the series I felt that some viewers watched and thought the cooking was marvellous but somehow not for them to try. I am very pleased to say that as the series has evolved over the years our MasterChef food has become more approachable, and I'm sure all of you cooks will want to rush out and try this year's recipes. I don't think that any of our contestants would ever want to be considered as pretentious prodigies of the kitchen. What makes their performance and consequently the programme so compelling and entertaining is the simple fact of real people cooking real food. As always, I should like to express my gratitude to our wonderful crew and production team, as well as to our talented contestants to whom this book is dedicated.

Loyd Grossman

NOTES FOR RECIPE USERS

Quantities are given in metric and imperial measures.
Follow one set of measurements only, not a combination,
because they are not interchangeable.

All spoon measures are level.

Fresh herbs are used unless otherwise stated.

Size 2 eggs are used unless otherwise suggested.

Ovens must be preheated to the temperature
specified in the recipe.

All recipes serve 4.

INTRODUCTION

Those who pour over the winning numbers in the National Lottery in the hope of improving their chances might do well, for a little light relief, to examine the statistics of MasterChef winners. For Marion MacFarlane, the new 1995 MasterChef is not only the third winner out of six to come from Scotland, but she is also the fourth teacher to carry off the trophy. I have always thought that there was a certain correlation between cooking and 'performing' in its broadest sense – most of the successful MasterChef entrants are pretty outgoing – but I had not imagined a direct link to the teaching profession.

What seems to be the case is that many of our best amateur cooks are those with extremely taxing careers for whom the calm of the kitchen and the creativity of cooking is their ultimate relaxation. In which case this book should offer instant access to these pleasures as it contains some of the most exciting and innovative recipes to come out of the red, yellow and blue kitchens in the six years of MasterChef.

The 1995 menus have stunned the judges not only with their originality but also their variety. From Beef and Mushroom Pudding to Cappuccino of Parsley with Pernod-seared Scallops, Salmon and Haddock Fish Cakes to Chocolate Gelato with Bitter Orange Sauce, the dishes have thrilled the tastebuds of Loyd Grossman's most discerning guests, and resulted in the 'judgely huddles', where deliberation and cogitation seem to take longer and longer.

Whether or not you have agreed with the judges' decisions, I hope that you, and those who share them with you, will enjoy the recipes which have made MasterChef 1995 such a hard fought and exciting series.

Finally I want to thank Loyd for his seemingly boundless energy and enthusiasm for everything to do with food. He has just built himself a wonderful new kitchen and I wish him many hours of pleasure in it. Loyd's accent may be an acquired taste, he may wave his arms about a bit, but he is always a joy for the crew and me to work with, and I thank him deeply for it.

RICHARD BRYAN
Producer and Director
MasterChef

THE MIDLANDS

GILL TUNKLE • JILL O'BRIEN • JOHN THORNBURN

PANEL OF JUDGES

Albert Roux • Cherie Lunghi • Loyd Grossman

WINNER

GILL TUNKLE'S MENU

STARTER

Warm Salad of Scallops in a Herb Butter Sauce

"The scallops were cooked to perfection" **Albert Roux**

MAIN COURSE

Fillet of Beef in Black Bean Sauce with Ginger and Coriander Crisps

Char-grilled Peppers

Timbale of Fragrant Wild Rice

"The meat was extremely good, a good combination of flavour" **Albert Roux**

DESSERT

Iced Passion Fruit Soufflé in a Caramel Cage,
with Glazed Strawberries and a Strawberry Coulis

"The passion fruit sorbet was incredible... wonderful, the texture... it was perfect" **Loyd**

Gill Tunkle comes from Coventry. She is PA to the chief executive of a major printing group, regularly visiting their many plants. Gill's hobbies include stencilling, and the walls of her home are covered with her works of art. Gill's fiancé, Peter, is in the process of building a replica Bugatti, and he and Gill are frequent visitors to the Bugatti Trust at Prescott.

WARM SALAD OF SCALLOPS IN A HERB BUTTER SAUCE

8 large shelled scallops with corals

Herb Butter Sauce:
125 g (4 oz) unsalted butter
1 egg yolk
1 small bunch each of fresh tarragon,
 parsley, chervil and chives, chopped
4 basil leaves, chopped
juice of ½ lemon
salt and freshly ground black pepper

To Serve:
4 handfuls of mixed salad leaves,
 (eg, frisée, lamb's lettuce, radicchio,
 rocket, watercress)

Clean and trim the whole scallops, then cut in half horizontally, retaining the coral. Place on a piece of kitchen paper in the refrigerator to firm up.

For the sauce, put the butter, egg yolk, herbs, lemon juice and a little seasoning in a food processor and process until the mixture becomes light in texture and colour.

Place the scallops in a single layer in a shallow ovenproof dish. Season with salt and pepper, then cover with the buttery herb mixture. Cook under a preheated grill for about 5 minutes until the sauce is bubbling and browned – by which time the scallops will be cooked. Check the seasoning.

Arrange 4 scallop halves in a circular pattern on each warmed serving plate with some of the sauce. Place a mound of mixed leaves in the centre of each plate. Drizzle a little more of the sauce over the top and serve at once.

Fillet of Beef in Black Bean Sauce

4 Aberdeen Angus fillet steaks, each about
  150 g (5 oz)
20 ml (4 tsp) fermented black beans
1 small garlic clove, peeled
4 cm (1½ inch) cube of fresh root ginger,
  peeled and roughly chopped
dash of rice wine
450 ml (15 fl oz) well-flavoured reduced
  beef stock
15 ml (1 tbsp) olive oil
60 ml (2 fl oz) red wine
salt and freshly ground black pepper

Ginger and Coriander Crisps:
150 g (5 oz) fresh root ginger
about 30 coriander leaves
sunflower oil for deep-frying

Trim the fillet steaks and set aside.

Rinse the fermented black beans well and pat dry with kitchen paper. Put half into a mortar. Add the garlic and ginger and pound with the pestle until smooth; the mixture should be quite dry and thick. Add a dash of rice wine and mix to a smooth paste. Warm the stock in a saucepan, then add the black bean paste. Turn off the heat and leave to infuse.

To make the ginger and coriander crisps, peel the ginger, cutting off any knobbly bits and trim to a good even shape. Slice extremely thinly across the diagonal to make 24-32 crisps. Rinse the coriander leaves and pat dry. Heat the oil for deep-frying to 160°C (325°F). Deep-fry the crisps in batches until golden, then drain on kitchen paper; they will crisp up as they cool. Deep-fry the coriander leaves for about 1 minute; do not overcook. Drain on kitchen paper.

To cook the steaks, heat the olive oil in a heavy-based pan or griddle. Add the steaks and cook for 3 minutes each side for medium rare. Remove from the pan and keep warm. Deglaze pan with the wine, then add the stock and black bean paste. Let bubble for a few moments, then strain and return to the pan. Add the whole black beans and check seasoning.

Carve each steak into 5mm (¼ inch) thick slices. Arrange on warmed plates and pour over the sauce. Sprinkle the ginger crisps and coriander leaves on top. Serve with the accompaniments.

Char-Grilled Peppers

1 red pepper
1 yellow pepper
olive oil, for brushing

Place the peppers under a preheated grill, turning frequently until tinged with brown. Whilst still hot, place in a tightly covered bowl and leave until cold.

Peel the skins off the peppers, then halve and remove the core and seeds. Rinse and pat dry. Cut each pepper half into 4 equal strips and thread onto skewers. Brush with a little olive oil and cook under a preheated grill until the edges are crispy and slightly charred.

Timbales of Fragrant Wild Rice

225 g (8 oz) easy-cook mixed long-grain and
  wild rice
salt
½ bunch of coriander

Bring a pan of salted water to the boil. Tie the coriander with string and add to the water. Bring to a rolling boil, then add the rice. Lower the heat and simmer gently for 15-18 minutes until al dente, cooked but still firm to the bite. Drain thoroughly, discarding the coriander.

Divide the rice between 4 warmed dariole moulds, level the surface, then unmould onto warmed serving plates.

ICED PASSION FRUIT SOUFFLÉ IN A CARAMEL CAGE

For the required quantity of juice you will need 8-10 ripe passion fruit. Halve the passion fruit, scoop out the seeds and pulp into a sieve over a bowl to strain the juice.

Soufflé:
2 eggs (size 3), separated
75 g (3 oz) icing sugar
90 ml (3 fl oz) passion fruit juice (see above)
250 ml (8 fl oz) double cream

Caramel Cages:
250 g (9 oz) caster sugar
50 ml (2 fl oz) liquid glucose
a little vegetable oil

To Decorate:
12 small strawberries
½ passion fruit

Strawberry Coulis:
125 g (4 oz) fresh strawberries
icing sugar, to taste

Whisk the egg yolks and half of the icing sugar together in a bowl, using an electric whisk if possible, until very pale and foamy. Add the passion fruit juice. In a separate bowl, whisk the egg whites until stiff, then whisk in the rest of the icing sugar. Whip the cream in another bowl until thick. Fold the passion fruit mixture into the whipped cream, then fold in the whisked egg white mixture.

Divide the mixture between 4 individual 150 ml (¼ pint) freezerproof moulds. Cover with cling film and freeze until firm.

For the caramel, dissolve the sugar in 90 ml (6 tbsp) water in a heavy-based pan over a low heat, then bring to the boil. Add the liquid glucose and cook until the syrup turns a pale caramel colour, ie until it registers 165°C (330°F)

on a sugar thermometer. Take off the heat and leave to rest for 2 minutes.

Meanwhile with your hand, spread the tiniest amount of oil over the back of a ladle. Dip a spoon into the caramel, let the excess run off then trickle the thread to and fro over the ladle to create a basket. Repeat this procedure if necessary, then gently twist the cage free. Repeat to make a further 3 cages and place into an airtight container. Do not leave them in a humid atmosphere, otherwise they will go sticky and collapse.

Dip the 12 strawberries for the decoration into the remaining caramel. If the caramel is too thick at this stage, gently reheat. Place the strawberries on non-stick baking parchment and keep in an airtight container.

To make the strawberry coulis, purée the strawberries in a blender or food processor, adding icing sugar to taste. Pass through a sieve into a bowl, cover and chill in the refrigerator until required.

About 30 minutes before serving, turn out the soufflés onto individual serving plates and place in the refrigerator to soften slightly while still retaining their shape. To serve, spoon the passion fruit pulp on top of the soufflés and cover each soufflé with a caramel cage. Place a spoonful of strawberry coulis to one side of the plate and top with 3 caramel strawberries. Serve immediately.

THE MIDLANDS

GILL TUNKLE • JILL O'BRIEN • JOHN THORNBURN

PANEL OF JUDGES

Albert Roux • Cherie Lunghi • Loyd Grossman

JILL O'BRIEN'S MENU

STARTER

Gingery Crab served on a Bed of Sweet Pears

"A lovely surprise... the crab with the pears, and very delicate" **Cherie Lunghi**

MAIN COURSE

Char-grilled Loin of Lamb Fillet
with Glazed Turnips, and a Cassis and Madeira Sauce

Sweet Potato Latkes

Mixed Peppers with Ground Coriander and Lemon Juice

"The lamb was beautifully cooked.
The whole dish was to me a revelation. It was fantastic" **Albert Roux**

DESSERT

Individual Chocolate and Rum Bombe,
served with Rum and Praline Cream

"A chocolate euphoria – gorgeous and beautifully presented" **Cherie Lunghi**

Jill O'Brien comes from Tenbury Wells in Worcestershire. She is a theatre sister at the local hospital, which has a well equipped and busy operating theatre. Jill is a keen rambler and spends much of her spare time with friends exploring the local hills and dales. Jill is also renowned for her homemade wines, prepared with elderberries and damsons picked fresh from her garden.

GINGERY CRAB SERVED ON A BED OF SWEET PEARS

1 dressed crab, weighing about 1.1 kg
  (2½ lb), shells reserved
50 ml (2 fl oz) olive oil
25 g (1 oz) fennel leaves
4 cardamom seeds
1 clove garlic, crushed
1 thyme sprig
1 large Provençal tomato, chopped
150 ml (¼ pint) medium white wine
15 g (½ oz) fresh root ginger, finely chopped
4 ripe pears
15 g (½ oz) butter
15 ml (1 tbsp) light brown sugar
150 ml (¼ pint) whipping cream
50 g (2 oz) Parmesan cheese, freshly grated
salt and freshly ground pepper
snipped chives, to garnish

Heat the oil in a large saucepan, add the crab shells and cook on a high heat for 3-4 minutes. Lower the heat and add the fennel, cardamom, garlic, thyme and tomato. Cook gently for a few minutes, then add the wine and 300 ml (½ pint) water. Simmer for 30 minutes.

Meanwhile, heat about 150 ml (¼ pint) water in a small pan. Add the ginger and cook for about 20 minutes, until tender. Drain and reserve.

Strain the stock and return to a clean pan. Boil steadily to reduce to approximately 90 ml (3 fl oz). Set aside.

Carefully peel and core the pears, then cut each one lengthwise into 4 pieces. Place in a casserole dish with the butter, brown sugar and 150 ml (¼ pint) water. Cover and poach gently in a preheated oven at 190°C (375°F) mark 5 for about 1 hour until tender. Keep warm.

Place the prepared crab meat in a saucepan and heat through gently over a low heat. Keep warm.

Pour the concentrated stock into another pan. Add the reserved ginger, the cream and the cooking juice from the pears. Heat the sauce through over a low heat, stirring.

Preheat the grill to high. Arrange 4 pear segments on each of 4 flameproof serving plates. Spoon the crab meat into the middle. Place a spoonful of sauce over the crab and spread the rest around the sides. Sprinkle the Parmesan over the crab. Place under a hot grill until lightly browned. Season with salt and pepper and serve immediately, garnished with chives.

CHAR-GRILLED LOIN OF LAMB FILLET WITH GLAZED TURNIPS AND A CASSIS AND MADEIRA SAUCE

Get your butcher to bone the lamb for you, remembering to ask for the bones which you will need for the sauce. For optimum flavour, allow the lamb to marinate overnight before cooking.

2 lamb loin fillets (plus reserved bones), total weight about 675 g (1½ lb)

Marinade:
180 ml (6 fl oz) red wine (eg Claret)
180 ml (6 fl oz) crème de cassis
juice of 1 lemon
1 large clove garlic, chopped
30 ml (2 tbsp) olive oil
few mixed herbs (eg bay leaf, parsley sprig, rosemary sprig)
1 tomato, chopped
salt and freshly ground black pepper

Sauce:
30 ml (2 tbsp) olive oil
reserved lamb bones
1 stick celery, with leaves
1 large carrot, chopped
1 medium onion, chopped
15 ml (1 tbsp) tomato purée
10 ml (2 tsp) Dijon mustard
50 ml (2 fl oz) Madeira
5 ml (1 tsp) redcurrant jelly
a little crème de cassis, to taste (optional)

Glazed Turnips:
4 turnips, sliced
5 ml (1 tsp) light brown sugar
30 ml (2 tbsp) crème de cassis
25 g (1 oz) butter
15 ml (1 tbsp) muscovado sugar

To Garnish:
herb sprigs
handful of blackcurrants, glazed in sugar syrup (optional)

Mix all the ingredients for the marinade together in a shallow dish. Add the lamb fillets and turn to coat. Cover and leave to marinate in a cool place overnight or for several hours at least.

The next day, remove the lamb from the marinade and set aside; reserve the marinade.

To prepare the sauce, heat the oil in a large saucepan. Add the lamb bones, celery, carrot and onion and fry, stirring, for a few minutes until browned; do not burn. Add the reserved marinade and 250 ml (8 fl oz) water. Bring to the boil and simmer for 30-45 minutes. Increase the heat and reduce the liquid by two thirds.

Meanwhile, prepare the glazed turnips. Put the turnips in a pan with 250 ml (8 fl oz) water, the light brown sugar, crème de cassis and seasoning. Bring to the boil, cover and cook for about 30 minutes until tender. Drain the turnips, adding the cooking liquor to the sauce. Add the butter and muscovado sugar to the turnips and toss over a moderate heat to glaze; keep warm.

When the sauce has reduced, remove from the heat and strain into another pan. Add the tomato purée, mustard, Madeira and redcurrant jelly. Check the seasoning and add a little more crème de cassis if needed; keep warm.

Meanwhile, preheat the grill to high (see note). Place the lamb on the grill rack and grill for 3-5 minutes each side, until browned on the outside but still pink in the middle.

To serve, thinly slice the lamb and arrange alternate pieces of lamb and turnip on the serving plate. Spoon around the sauce and garnish with herbs and glazed blackcurrants if desired.

Note: If you have a griddle, use it in preference to the grill for cooking the lamb for a char-grilled effect.

SWEET POTATO LATKES

1 large sweet potato, about 225 g (8 oz)
2 large potatoes, each about 225 g (8 oz)
2 eggs, beaten
50 g (2 oz) plain flour, sifted
15 ml (1 tbsp) chopped onion
salt and freshly ground black pepper
50 ml (2 fl oz) oil

Peel all of the potatoes and immerse them in a bowl of cold water. Leave to soak for 1 hour. Drain and coarsely grate the potatoes. Add the eggs, flour and chopped onion. Mix thoroughly, seasoning with salt and pepper.

Heat the oil in a frying pan until it is quite hot. Place tablespoonfuls of the mixture in the pan, spacing them apart. Cook on one side for about 5 minutes until crisp and brown underneath, then turn and cook the other side for approximately 5 minutes until cooked through and brown and crispy on both sides. Serve piping hot.

MIXED PEPPERS WITH GROUND CORIANDER AND LEMON JUICE

1 red pepper
1 green pepper
1 yellow pepper
1 orange pepper
15 ml (1 tbsp) lemon juice
25 g (1 oz) butter
15 ml (1 tbsp) coriander seeds, finely ground
pinch of sugar, to taste

Halve the peppers, remove the core and seeds, then thinly slice the flesh. Bring a pan of salted water to the boil. Add the peppers and simmer for 1-2 minutes only. Drain and toss with the lemon juice, butter, coriander and sugar to taste. Serve at once.

INDIVIDUAL CHOCOLATE AND RUM BOMBE, SERVED WITH RUM AND PRALINE CREAM

Praline:
50 g (2 oz) unblanched almonds
50 g (2 oz) caster sugar

Chocolate Bombes:
250 g (9 oz) plain chocolate
50 g (2 oz) unsalted butter
60-90 ml (4-6 tbsp) rum, to taste
200 ml (7 fl oz) double cream, lightly whipped

Rum and Praline Cream:
300 ml (½ pint) double cream
25 g (1 oz) praline (see method)
15 ml (1 tbsp) rum, or to taste

To Decorate:
chocolate leaves or curls

Place four 150 ml (¼ pint) individual moulds in the refrigerator to chill thoroughly.

To make the praline, place the almonds and sugar in a heavy-based pan over a low heat until the sugar melts and turns a nut-brown colour. Immediately remove from the heat and pour into an oiled shallow baking tin. Leave to cool until set hard. When set hard, remove from the dish and grind to a powder in a food processor or blender.

For the chocolate bombes, break up the chocolate and put it into a pan with 90 ml (3 fl oz) water. Place over a gentle heat until melted to the consistency of a thick cream. Remove the pan from the heat. Cream the butter in a bowl, then add the melted chocolate and rum to taste. Gradually beat in three quarters of the praline, then fold in the cream. Divide the mixture between the chilled moulds and leave in the refrigerator for approximately 2 hours until set.

For the rum and praline cream, whip the cream very lightly, adding the praline and rum.

To serve, dip the moulds quickly into hot water and invert on to individual serving plates to release the bombes. Spoon the praline cream around each bombe. Decorate with chocolate leaves or curls and serve at once.

THE MIDLANDS

GILL TUNKLE • JILL O'BRIEN • JOHN THORNBURN

PANEL OF JUDGES

Albert Roux • Cherie Lunghi • Loyd Grossman

JOHN THORNBURN'S MENU

STARTER

*Cotswold Trout on a Compote of Roasted Tomatoes
with a Red Onion, Black Olive and Pesto Sauce*

"Hearty cooking. Beautifully executed.
Beautiful pink fish... a very nice dish" **Albert Roux**

MAIN COURSE

Breast of Herefordshire Wood Pigeon with Chinese Spices

Caramelised Carrots

Cabbage with Sesame Seeds

Fried New Potatoes with Spring Onions

"Delicious. Very rich, but not too gamey" **Cherie Lunghi**

DESSERT

*Warm, Upside-down Prune and Apple Cake,
served with a Prune and Armagnac Ice Cream*

"Delicious, wonderfully liquered,
and rich in an interesting and warm way" **Cherie Lunghi**

John Thornburn lives in Ledbury, Herefordshire. John represents up and coming motor racing drivers – even Nigel Mansell was once on his books! His latest venture is importing personally selected wines from the vineyards of France. After work there is nothing John enjoys more than a round of golf at the Ross-on-Wye Club with his friends.

COTSWOLD TROUT ON A COMPOTE OF ROASTED TOMATOES WITH RED ONION, BLACK OLIVE AND PESTO SAUCE

4 trout fillets, each about 200 g (7 oz)
120 ml (4 fl oz) extra-virgin olive oil
1 clove garlic, chopped
100 g (3½ oz) red onion, chopped
juice of 1 lemon
30 ml (2 tbsp) white wine
50 g (2 oz) stoned black olives, chopped
6 plum tomatoes
sea salt and freshly ground black pepper
10 ml (2 tsp) oil
20 g (¾ oz) basil leaves, shredded
12 coriander seeds
pinch of sugar

Basil Sauce:
50 g (2 oz) basil leaves
150 ml (¼ pint) extra-virgin olive oil
1 clove garlic
25 g (1 oz) pine nuts
20 g (¾ oz) Parmesan cheese, freshly grated
sea salt and freshly ground black pepper

First make the basil sauce: put all of the ingredients in a blender or food processor and work until smooth; set aside.

Heat the olive oil in a pan, add the garlic and onion and fry gently for 3 minutes. Add the lemon juice, wine and olives and cook for 4 minutes. Dice two of the plum tomatoes and add to the pan. Season with salt and pepper to taste, remove from the heat and allow to cool.

Halve the other 4 tomatoes and remove their seeds. Place in a pan with the 10 ml (2 tsp) oil and cook on a high heat for 1-2 minutes until lightly coloured. Transfer to a shallow baking tin, sprinkle with the shredded basil, coriander seeds, salt, pepper and sugar.

Spoon about a third of the onion and olive mixture into another baking tin and place the trout on top. Season with salt and pepper and spoon on the rest of the onion and olive mixture.

Place the tomatoes and trout in a preheated oven at 230°C (450°F) mark 8 for 4 minutes. Arrange the tomatoes on warmed serving plates and place the trout on top. Add the pan juices from the tomatoes to the onion and olive mixture. Sprinkle this over and around the trout and drizzle with the basil sauce. Sprinkle with sea salt and pepper. Serve at once.

BREAST OF HEREFORD WOOD PIGEON WITH CHINESE SPICES

4 wood pigeons
30 ml (2 tbsp) oil
Chinese spice mixture (see right)

Sauce:
reserved pigeon carcasses
15 ml (1 tbsp) oil
60 g (2 oz) shallots, chopped
3 cloves garlic, chopped
15 g (1½ oz) fresh root ginger, chopped
60 g (2 oz) mushrooms, chopped
1 thyme sprig
2 tomatoes, chopped
60 ml (4 tbsp) red wine vinegar
100 ml (3½ fl oz) red wine
15 g (½ oz) honey
5 ml (1 tsp) soy sauce
30 g (1 oz) butter

Remove the breasts from the pigeons, using a sharp knife. Rub all over with Chinese spice mixture to taste and set aside.

To make the sauce, roughly chop the pigeon carcasses. Heat the oil in a heavy-based pan, add the pigeon bones and brown over a moderate heat. Add the shallots, garlic, ginger and mushrooms. Sauté until lightly browned. Add the thyme and tomatoes; cook for 2 minutes. Add the vinegar and cook until almost completely evaporated. Add the wine and allow to bubble until reduced by half. Add the honey, soy sauce and 400 ml (14 fl oz) water. Simmer for about 1½ hours until reduced by half.

Strain the sauce through a fine sieve into a clean pan. Reheat, whisking in the butter a little at a time.

To cook the pigeon breasts, heat the oil in a heavy-based frying pan. Add the pigeon breasts and cook over a high heat for 4 minutes. Turn and cook the other side for 2½ minutes. Transfer to warmed serving plates and surround with the sauce. Serve with the accompaniments.

Chinese Spice Mixture: Mix equal quantities of grated galangal, star anise, cloves, ground ginger, ground cinnamon, ground nutmeg, celery salt, ground coriander, allspice, dried black beans and dried orange peel. Grind to a powder, using a spice grinder or blender. Store in an airtight jar and use as required.

FRIED NEW POTATOES WITH SPRING ONIONS

8 new potatoes
salt
60 ml (4 tbsp) oil
30 g (1 oz) butter
8 spring onions, chopped

Cook the potatoes in their skins in boiling salted water until almost tender. Drain and slice. Heat the oil and butter in a pan and add the sliced potatoes. Cook, turning, until golden. Season with salt and pepper and add the spring onions. Cook for 1 minute. Remove from the pan and drain on kitchen paper. Serve at once.

CARAMELISED CARROTS

4 carrots, peeled
salt
15 g (½ oz) fresh root ginger, shredded
30 g (1 oz) butter
20 g (4 tsp) sugar

Slice the carrots on the diagonal. Add to a pan of salted water with half of the ginger. Bring to the boil, lower the heat and simmer for about 4 minutes until barely cooked. Drain and allow to cool.

When ready to serve, melt the butter in a frying pan, then add the sugar and a splash of water. Heat until the sugar is dissolved, then add the carrots and remaining ginger. Cook until the carrots are tender and lightly coloured.

CABBAGE WITH SESAME SEEDS

200 g (7 oz) cabbage (eg Savoy), cored
salt and freshly ground black pepper
30 g (1 oz) butter
20 ml (4 tsp) sesame oil
5 ml (1 tsp) sesame seeds, toasted

Cut the cabbage into squares and cook in boiling salted water for 4 minutes. Drain and refresh under cold running water. Set aside until ready to serve. When needed, heat the butter in a frying pan with the sesame oil. Add the cabbage, season with salt and pepper and toss until warmed through. Arrange on warmed side plates and sprinkle with the toasted sesame seeds.

WARM UPSIDE-DOWN PRUNE AND APPLE CAKE WITH A PRUNE AND ARMAGNAC ICE CREAM

For this recipe you will need prunes bottled in armagnac flavoured syrup, which must be prepared well in advance (see note).

Prune and Apple Cake:

2 Granny Smith's apples
65 g (2½ oz) butter
90 g (3¼ oz) caster sugar
1 vanilla pod, split
grated rind of 1 orange
70 g (2½ oz) flour
pinch of salt
2.5 ml (½ tsp) baking powder
juice of ½ orange
40 g (1½ oz) ground almonds
100 ml (3½ fl oz) milk
1 egg
100 g (3½ oz) prunes in armagnac, drained
   and stoned

Ice Cream:

200 ml (⅓ pint) milk
300 ml (½ pint) double cream
1 vanilla pod, split
8 egg yolks
80 g (3 oz) caster sugar
200 g (7 oz) prunes in armagnac, drained,
   stoned and chopped
75 g (3 oz) syrup from prunes
75 ml (5 tbsp) armagnac

For the ice cream, put the milk in a heavy-based pan with the cream and vanilla pod. Slowly bring to the boil over a low heat. Meanwhile, whisk the egg yolks and sugar together in a bowl until well mixed. Pour on the hot milk, whisking constantly, then pour back into the pan. Cook over a very low heat, stirring continuously, until the custard is thick enough to coat the back of the spoon; do not allow to boil. Strain through a fine sieve into a bowl. Stir in the syrup from the prunes.

Transfer to an ice cream machine and churn for a few minutes, then add the chopped prunes and armagnac. Churn for approximately 45 minutes until firm. (If you do not have an ice cream machine freeze in a suitable container, stirring two or three times during freezing.)

To make the prune and apple cake, peel the apples and cut each one into 8 wedges, discarding the core. Melt 15 g (½ oz) of the butter in a pan. Add 20 g (¾ oz) sugar with the apples. Cook over a high heat for about 3 minutes until softened and beginning to caramelise.

Cream the remaining butter and sugar together in a bowl until light and fluffy. Scrape the seeds from the vanilla pod and add to the mixture with the orange rind. Sift the flour, salt and baking powder together onto the mixture and stir in. Add the orange juice, ground almonds, milk and egg. Mix until smooth and creamy.

Arrange the apple and prunes in greased individual 10 cm (4 inch) tart tins. Spoon the cake mixture over the top and place the tins on a baking sheet. Cook in a preheated oven at 200°C (400°F) mark 6 for 15 minutes. Invert the cakes onto individual serving plates, add a scoop of ice cream and serve at once.

Note: To prepare the prunes in armagnac, first make a sugar syrup. Dissolve 450 g (1 lb) sugar in 1 litre (1¾ pints) water in a heavy-based pan, then add the juice of 1 orange, 2 split vanilla pods, 1 cinnamon stick and 3 tea bags. Bring to the boil and boil for 5 minutes. Discard the tea bags. Add 1.5 kg (3½ lb) prunes, return to the boil and simmer for 3 minutes. Transfer to a sterilised preserving jar. Allow to cool then cover, seal and leave in a cool place for 3 days. Pour off half of the sugar syrup and top up with Armagnac. Re-seal and leave in a cool place for at least 3 months before use.

SCOTLAND & NORTHERN IRELAND

MARION MACFARLANE • LINDA DOHERTY • MICHAEL GRAY

PANEL OF JUDGES

Paul Reed • Sandi Toksvig • Loyd Grossman

WINNER

MARION MACFARLANE'S MENU

STARTER

*Scallop Mousseline inlaid with Crab served
with Little Tartlets of Jerusalem Artichoke Purée*

"That was very good, you could taste the crab and the mousse was light" **Paul Reed**

MAIN COURSE

Fillet of Highland Hare with Wild Mushrooms in a Creamy Marsala Sauce

Forcemeat Balls

Stir-fried Leeks

Clapshot with Fresh herbs

Hot Grated Beetroot

"I thought that was delicious, absolutely delicious" **Sandi Toksvig**

DESSERT

Pears poached in Elderflower Syrup, with Blackcurrant Sorbet

"They married very well, the combination of flavours there" **Paul Reed**

Marion MacFarlane comes from Newtonhill in Kincardinshire, Scotland. Marion is a primary school teacher in the rural village of Mary Culter, and enjoys passing on her creativity and love of food to the children. Her leisure pursuits include wine-tasting and she meets up regularly with the other members of the Newtonhill Imbibers.

SCALLOP MOUSSELINE INLAID WITH CRAB

50-75 g (2-3 oz) white crabmeat (including
small pieces of coral roe – if available)
210 g (7½ oz) cleaned scallops with corals
(see note)
5 ml (1 tsp) salt
freshly ground white pepper
1 egg (size 3)
150 ml (¼ pint) double cream
90 ml (3 fl oz) soured cream

To Serve:
Tartlets of Artichoke Purée (see right)
crab claw tips (optional)
herb sprigs, to garnish

Put the scallops into a food processor, add the salt and pepper and work until smooth. Add the egg and process for 1 minute. Transfer to a bowl, cover and chill for at least 30 minutes. Gradually fold in the cream and soured cream.

Butter 4 dariole moulds or ramekins and divide half of the scallop mousseline between them. Spoon the white crab meat in a layer on top, placing a small piece of coral in the centre (if available). Top with the rest of the scallop mousseline. Settle the mixture by bumping the moulds gently on the work surface. Cover each with a circle of greaseproof paper. Put a folded newspaper in the bottom of a roasting tin and stand the moulds on top. Add enough hot water to come halfway up the sides of the moulds. Bake in a preheated oven at 180°C (350°F) mark 4 for 25 minutes.

To serve, allow the mousselines to stand for a few minutes. Carefully unmould onto one side of the plate and decorate with the small tips of crab claw. Arrange the warm artichoke tartlet on the other side and decorate the plate with small pieces of crab coral (if available) and fresh herbs.

Note: This quantity is the weight of the scallops after cleaning. If you prepare them yourself, reserve the frills to make a stock for cooking the artichokes.

LITTLE TARTLETS OF JERUSALEM ARTICHOKE PURÉE

Pastry:
50 g (2 oz) plain flour
pinch of salt
25 g (1 oz) butter
10 ml (2 tsp) water (approximately)

Artichoke Purée:
225 g (8 oz) Jerusalem artichokes, peeled
reserved frills from scallops (see notes above
and right)
salt and freshly ground black pepper
dash of lemon juice

To make the pastry, sift the flour and salt into a bowl. Rub in the butter until the mixture resembles fine breadcrumbs. Add sufficient water to bind the dough. Wrap in cling film and leave to rest in the refrigerator for 30 minutes.

For the filling, simmer the scallop frills in about 150 ml (¼ pint) water for about 20 minutes to make a stock; strain into a clean pan. Add the Jerrusalem artichokes to this stock and simmer for about 15 minutes.

Drain the artichokes and place in a blender or food processor with a little of the stock. Work to a smooth purée. Add seasoning and a dash of lemon juice to taste.

Roll out the pastry thinly and use to line barquettes or other small decorative moulds. Prick the bases with a fork. Line with baking beans and bake blind in a preheated oven at 190°C (375°F) mark 5 for 10 minutes. Remove the beans.

Just before serving, spoon in the warm artichoke purée. Serve at once.

Note: Alternatively you could use a light fish stock made by using fish bones (eg plaice or sole).

FILLET OF HIGHLAND HARE WITH WILD MUSHROOMS IN A CREAMY MARSALA SAUCE

Depending on the season I sometimes use a mixture of wild mushrooms, such as chanterelles, boletus, pied de mouton, and cultivated mushrooms. If wild mushrooms are unavailable I use chestnut mushrooms and add 25 g (1 oz) of dried ceps, soaked in warm water for 30 minutes, then drained. It is essential to use a young hare. Remember that you will need to marinate the fillets for 24 hours before cooking.

2 saddles of hare
10 ml (2 tsp) hazelnut oil
8 dried morels
175 g (6 oz) mixed mushrooms (see above)
salt and freshly ground black pepper
10 ml (2 tsp) olive oil
40 g (1½ oz) unsalted butter
300 ml (½ pint) hare stock
120 ml (4 fl oz) Marsala
150 ml (¼ pint) double cream

To Serve:
forcemeat balls
chervil sprigs

Carefully remove the fillets and the tiny fillets mignon from the saddles of hare, reserving the carcasses to make the stock. Place the meat in a shallow dish, drizzle with the hazelnut oil and rub in. Leave to marinate for about 24 hours. Trim the ends off the fillets; reserve the trimmings and the fillets mignon for the forcemeat balls (see overleaf).

The next day soak the dried morels in warm water to cover for 30 minutes; drain, straining and reserving a little of the liquid. Slice all of the fresh mushrooms and set aside. Season the hare fillets with salt and pepper. Heat the oil and a knob of butter in a frying pan. When hot, add the hare fillets and sear on both sides over a high heat for 3-5 minutes, depending on size; the fillets should still be quite pink. Remove and keep warm.

Pour off the fat then add the remaining butter to the pan and sauté the fresh mushrooms for a few minutes. Season with salt and pepper, remove from the pan and keep warm. Add the stock and reserved morel soaking liquid. Reduce almost by half, then add the Marsala and reduce again. When the alcohol has evaporated, add the cream and reduce until the sauce thickens. Add the morels and heat through.

To serve, carve the hare fillets into 6-7 collops and arrange on warmed serving plates in a circle around a mound of stir-fried leeks. Garnish with the mixed mushrooms and spoon over the sauce. Position a forcemeat ball on the leeks and garnish the plates with sprigs of chervil.

Forcemeat Balls

I use the fillet mignons and the ends trimmed from the hare fillets to make these.

50 g (2 oz) reserved hare meat (see page 25)
50 g (2 oz) chestnut mushrooms
7.5 ml (1½ tsp) double cream
salt and freshly ground black pepper

Put the hare meat and mushrooms in a food processor and process until finely chopped. Mix with the cream and season with salt and pepper. Divide into 4 equal portions and roll into balls. Cover and keep in a cool place until needed.

Bake the forcemeat balls in a preheated oven at 190°C (375°F) mark 5 for 5-6 minutes until set. Serve with the hare.

Stir-fried Leeks

2 small leeks
sunflower oil, for frying

Slice the leeks into rounds and wash well. Drain thoroughly. Heat a little oil in a wok or frying pan, add the leeks and stir-fry for 2-3 minutes until just cooked. Serve at once.

Clapshot with Fresh Herbs

This is a traditional Scottish dish of "chappit neeps and tatties", or mashed swede and potatoes. The addition of herbs and olive oil transforms it into a wonderful 90's dish.

450 g (1 lb) potatoes
350 g (12 oz) swede
salt
25 g (1 oz) butter
25 ml (1 fl oz) virgin olive oil
15 ml (1 tbsp) finely chopped chives
15 ml (1 tbsp) finely chopped parsley
10 ml (2 tsp) finely chopped celery leaves
   (see note)
freshly grated nutmeg, to taste

Cut the potatoes and swede into 2.5 cm (1 inch) cubes. Place in a saucepan and add water to cover. Bring to the boil and cook until soft. Drain well and mash until smooth. Add the butter, olive oil, herbs and celery leaves. Sprinkle with grated nutmeg to serve.

Note: When lovage is in season, use it in preference to celery leaves.

Hot Grated Beetroot

2 boiled beetroot
25 g (1 oz) butter
2.5 ml (½ tsp) sugar
5 ml (1 tsp) red wine vinegar, or to taste
salt and freshly ground black pepper

Remove the skin from the beetroot, then grate, using a medium grater. Melt the butter in a pan, add the beetroot and heat through. Add the sugar and vinegar to taste. Season with salt and pepper to taste.

PEARS POACHED IN ELDERFLOWER SYRUP

2 firm pears (Comice or William)
30 ml (2 tbsp) sugar
dash of lemon juice
45 ml (3 tbsp) elderflower cordial

To Serve:
Blackcurrant Sorbet (see right)
elderflowers, borage or mint sprigs,
*   to decorate*

Put the sugar, lemon juice and elder-flower cordial into a pan with about 300 ml (½ pint) water. Dissolve over a low heat, then bring to the boil. Peel, halve and remove the cores from the pears. Add the pears to the syrup and poach gently until just tender; do not allow to boil. Carefully transfer the pears to a bowl and cover with the syrup. Leave to cool. When needed, slice length-wise, leaving the stalk end intact and fan out on kitchen paper.

To serve, place the fanned pear on one side of each serving plate and place a scoop of blackcurrant sorbet alongside. Decorate with elderflowers, borage or mint to serve.

BLACKCURRANT SORBET

If, like me, you are fond of blackcurrants, this full-flavoured fruity sorbet is definitely the one for you! For optimum effect serve it in a rose petal cup, remembering to remove the bitter part at the base of each petal.

175 g (6 oz) granulated sugar
275 g (9 oz) blackcurrants
15 ml (1 tbsp) crème de cassis
dash of lemon juice

First make a stock syrup by dissolving the sugar in 300 ml (½ pint) over a low heat, then simmer for 5 minutes. Remove from the heat and allow to cool.

Purée the blackcurrants in a blender or food processor, then pass through a nylon sieve to remove the pips. Stir in the cooled syrup, cassis, and lemon juice to taste. Cool and then churn in an ice-cream maker until ready. Transfer to a suitable container and freeze until required.

Note: If you do not have an ice-cream machine, freeze the sorbet in a suitable container, whisking periodically during freezing to break down the ice crystals and ensure an even-textured result.

SCOTLAND & NORTHERN IRELAND

MARION MACFARLANE • LINDA DOHERTY • MICHAEL GRAY

PANEL OF JUDGES
Paul Reed • Sandi Toksvig • Loyd Grossman

LINDA DOHERTY'S MENU

STARTER
Pyramids of Salmon and Mango Salsa with Irish Mist Flambéed Prawns

"I thought the mango salsa was excellent" **Loyd**

MAIN COURSE
*Home Smoked County Antrim Fillet of Lamb and Garden Herbs
with a Juniper and Lavender Sauce*

Mixed Grains

Selection of Seasonal Vegetables

"I thought the lamb was just fabulous,
and I loved the mixed grains, because I'm an old hippie" **Loyd**

DESSERT
Irish Goat's Milk Cheese Trinity with Strawberry Coulis

"The dessert, well, it was lovely, beautiful, so clean, so tasty
and uncomplicated" **Paul Reed**

L inda Doherty comes from Belfast. A medical technical officer,
Linda is currently learning the intricacies of reflexology. Her
own reflexes are regularly sharpened up with some punishing
aerobics! In quieter relaxation mode, Linda settles down
to her elaborate and colourful tapestry.

PYRAMIDS OF SALMON AND MANGO SALSA WITH IRISH MIST FLAMBÉED PRAWNS

450 g (1 lb) salmon fillets, skinned
12 large cooked prawns in shells
45 ml (3 tbsp) coriander leaves, finely chopped
finely grated rind and juice of 1 lime
7.5 ml (1½ tsp) olive oil

Mango Salsa:
1 small mango
2.5 cm (1 inch) piece fresh root ginger, peeled and finely chopped
2 spring onions, finely chopped
freshly ground black pepper
dash of lime juice, to taste
22 ml (1½ tbsp) Irish Mist (see note)

To Garnish:
coriander leaves

Cut the salmon fillets into four 7.5 cm (3 inch) circles, four 5 cm (2 inch) circles and four 2.5 cm (1 inch) circles, removing any fine bones with tweezers.

Place the salmon rounds in a large shallow glass or ceramic dish, together with the prawns. Mix together the chopped coriander, lime rind and juice, and the olive oil. Pour over the fish, cover and leave to marinate for 20 minutes, turning occasionally.

Meanwhile prepare the mango salsa. Peel the mango and cut the flesh away from the stone. Dice the mango flesh finely. Place in a bowl and add the ginger and spring onions. Season with a little black pepper and add a little lime juice to taste.

Remove the salmon and prawns from the marinade. Lay the salmon rounds in a microproof dish and microwave on HIGH for 1-1½ minutes until just cooked. (If you do not have a microwave, cook under a preheated grill or pan-fry in a little butter and oil until just cooked.)

To serve, place the 4 largest salmon rounds on individual serving plates. Spoon a little mango salsa on top and carefully level out. Cover with the medium-sized rounds. Spoon on more mango salsa, then top with the smallest salmon rounds to form pyramids.

Preheat a griddle or heavy-based frying pan, add the prawns and heat through. Pour in the Irish Mist and set alight. Once the flames have died down, arrange the prawns around the salmon pyramids. Garnish with coriander and serve warm or cold.

Note: Irish Mist is a liqueur made from Irish Whiskey and heather honey.

HOME SMOKED COUNTY ANTRIM FILLET OF LAMB AND GARDEN HERBS WITH A JUNIPER AND LAVENDER SAUCE

1 county Antrim fillet of lamb (cut from the tenderloin, 5 chops long-boned)
15 ml (1 tbsp) Irish country honey
1 clove garlic, crushed
15 ml (1 tbsp) each finely chopped rosemary, thyme, chives and parsley
freshly ground black pepper

Sauce:
lamb bones and lean scraps of meat from loin
15 ml (1 tbsp) olive oil
2-3 shallots (unpeeled), halved
¼ small carrot
few thyme sprigs
6 juniper berries
1 head of lavender flowers
1 glass Madeira
30 ml (2 tbsp) redcurrant jelly

To Smoke:
125 g (4 oz) rice
mahogany wood shavings and herb trimmings

To Garnish:
coriander sprigs
chives

Carefully remove the fillet from the loin of lamb, reserving the bones and trimmings. Trim off all fat and gristle. Rub the honey and crushed garlic into the meat. Mix all the herbs together, season with pepper and press firmly onto the surface of the lamb. Wrap in foil and keep in a cool place until ready to smoke; do not refrigerate.

To prepare the sauce, heat the oil in a saucepan. Add the shallots, carrot, lamb bones and scraps of meat, and the thyme sprigs. Crush the juniper berries lightly and add to the pan with the lavender flowers. Brown the meat well, then add the Madeira together with about 120 ml (4 fl oz) water. Reduce by about one quarter, then strain through a fine sieve into a clean saucepan. Add the redcurrant jelly and reduce to half of the original volume. Remove any fat from the surface and check the seasoning. Keep warm.

Double line an old saucepan or wok with foil. Scatter the rice and a few mahogany wood shavings over the base. Place a metal rack on top. Carefully lay the meat on the rack. Cover with a lid and seal the rim with foil. Place the saucepan on a high heat for 5 minutes.

Remove the meat from the pan and check how rare it is. Wrap in foil and bake in a preheated oven at 200°C (400°F) mark 6 for 10-15 minutes for rare, 15-20 minutes for medium to well done, (depending on the original smoking). Leave to rest for a few minutes.

To serve, slice the lamb thinly and serve on a bed of mixed grains on warmed individual serving plates. Spoon a little sauce over the lamb and garnish with coriander and chives. Serve immediately, with seasonal vegetables.

MIXED GRAINS

50 g (2 oz) wheat berries
50 g (2 oz) wild rice
25 g (1 oz) long-grain white rice
salt and freshly ground black pepper

Place the wheat berries in a heavy-based saucepan. Pour in sufficient water to cover and bring to the boil. Cover and cook for 15 minutes, then add the wild rice and cook for a further 20 minutes, adding more water to the pan as necessary. Finally add the white rice and salt to taste. Cook for 10 minutes or until all of the grains are just tender and the water is absorbed. Check the seasoning before serving, with the lamb.

IRISH GOAT'S MILK CHEESE TRINITY WITH STRAWBERRY COULIS

You will need to partially prepare this dessert the day before it is required, unless you buy the goat's yogurt rather than make it yourself.

600 ml (1 pint) fresh goat's milk
15 ml (1 tbsp) live yogurt culture (see note)
1 vanilla pod, split
50 g (2 oz) each of 3 different soft fruits (eg strawberries, raspberries, redcurrants), or unshelled nuts (eg hazelnuts)

Strawberry Coulis:
125 g (4 oz) strawberries

To Serve:
extra soft fruit
mint sprigs
icing sugar, for dusting

Put half of the goat's milk in a saucepan and bring to boiling point. Remove from the heat and allow to cool until lukewarm (ie blood temperature – 37°C [98.4°F]). Stir in the live yogurt culture and pour into a warmed vacuum flask. Set aside overnight.

The following day, put the remaining 300 ml (½ pint) milk in a heavy-based saucepan. Add the split vanilla pod and heat gently to boiling point. Add the yogurt, remove from the heat and stir once; soft curds will form.

Set a colander lined with muslin over a bowl. Pour in the milk curds. Allow to drain and cool for 10-15 minutes. Carefully gather up the muslin and squeeze out as much liquid whey as possible. Place a small flat plate on top of the muslin-wrapped cheese, then place a weight on top. Leave in the refrigerator for 1 hour.

Meanwhile make the strawberry coulis by pressing the strawberries through a fine nylon sieve into a bowl. Set aside.

Prepare the soft fruit and cut into small pieces, if necessary. Roast the nuts in their shells by microwaving on HIGH for 2 minutes. Shell and crush the nuts. Alternatively, shell the nuts and toast under a preheated grill.

Divide the cheese into three equal portions and mix each one with a chosen variety of soft fruit or roasted nuts.

Line 12 small moulds, about 25-50 ml (1-2 fl oz) capacity with muslin. Fill with the flavoured cheeses to make 4 moulds of each flavour. Cover with another piece of muslin and press down firmly. Chill in the refrigerator for about 1 hour. Remove the cheese moulds from the refrigerator 30 minutes before serving and allow to come to room temperature.

To serve, turn out three different fruit cheeses onto each individual serving plate. Spoon the strawberry coulis around the cheeses and decorate with extra soft fruit and mint sprigs. Dust with icing sugar just before serving.

Note: For convenience you can buy goat's yogurt rather than make your own.

—— SCOTLAND & NORTHERN IRELAND ——

MARION MACFARLANE • LINDA DOHERTY • MICHAEL GRAY

PANEL OF JUDGES

Paul Reed • Sandi Toksvig • Loyd Grossman

MICHAEL GRAY'S MENU

STARTER

Steamed Leeks with Bacon and a Tomato and Coriander Sauce

"I thought it was delicious" **Sandi Toksvig**

MAIN COURSE

Poached Fillet of Salmon with a Citrus Sauce,
served with Fresh Dates and a Fettucine of Vegetables

"The subtleness of the date with the lightness of the salmon
went very, very well" **Paul Reed**

DESSERT

Orange Almond Tart with Ginger and Honey Ice Cream

"The tart was good. The pastry was super" **Paul Reed**

Originally from Ireland, Michael now lives and works in Edinburgh. He has recently qualified as a doctor. Michael is a hardy sportsman and water-skis at the Scottish National Club in all weathers.

Steamed Leeks with Bacon and a Tomato and Coriander Sauce

450 g (1 lb) baby cherry tomatoes
45 ml (3 tbsp) olive oil
5 ml (1 tsp) caster sugar
salt and freshly ground black pepper
900 g (2 lb) leeks, thoroughly cleaned
50 g (2 oz) butter
2 turnips
60 ml (2 fl oz) white wine
15 ml (1 tbsp) finely chopped coriander
  leaves
225 g (8 oz) lightly smoked bacon, cut into
  lardons
cayenne pepper, to taste

Arrange the cherry tomatoes in a shallow ovenproof dish and add 15 ml (1 tbsp) of the oil, the sugar and 2.5 ml (½ tsp) salt. Toss the tomatoes to ensure they are evenly coated. Bake in a preheated oven at 220°C (425°F) mark 7 for 30-40 minutes until the tomatoes begin to blacken and have released plenty of juice. Allow to cool in the dish.

Meanwhile prepare the leeks. Slice into 5 cm (2 inch) lengths and steam over boiling water for up to 12 minutes, depending on thickness, until just cooked, but still retaining some crispness. Transfer to a shallow dish and dot with the butter. Season with salt and pepper to taste; keep warm.

Peel the turnips, slice into fine julienne strips and place in a bowl of iced water.

For the sauce, press the cherry tomatoes through a conical sieve into a pan to remove the seeds and skin and yield a tomato coulis. Add the wine and bring to the boil. Allow to reduce for 1-2 minutes, then remove from the heat and add the chopped coriander. Keep warm.

To serve, heat the remaining oil in a pan and quickly fry the bacon lardons until tender and slightly browned. Drain on kitchen paper. Using a 7.5 cm (3 inch) pastry cutter as a guide, arrange a round of turnip julienne in the centre of each plate. Slice the leek sections lengthwise into quarters and arrange these on top of the turnips in a stack. Pour the sauce around each stack and scatter the bacon lardons on the sauce. Sprinkle a little cayenne pepper over the leeks and garnish each serving with a tomato flower if you like. Serve at once.

Note: To make a tomato flower, simply peel the skin from an unripe tomato, retaining a uniformly thick and intact skin. Roll the skin into a flower shape.

POACHED FILLET OF SALMON WITH A CITRUS SAUCE, SERVED WITH FRESH DATES AND A FETTUCINE OF VEGETABLES

If possible, obtain salmon fillets cut from the middle of the fish for this dish.

4 salmon fillets, each about 175-225 g
  (6-8 oz)
salt and freshly ground white pepper

Pasta:
175 g (6 oz) plain flour
3 eggs (size 3), lightly beaten
15 ml (1 tbsp) oil
2.5 ml (½ tsp) salt

Vegetables:
4 large carrots, peeled
4 courgettes
25 g (1 oz) butter

Sauce:
50 g (2 oz) butter
2 shallots, finely chopped
120 ml (4 fl oz) white wine
120 ml (4 fl oz) fish stock
60 ml (2 fl oz) double cream
juice of 1 lemon, to taste

To Garnish:
6-8 fresh dates, stoned and sliced
tarragon sprigs

First make the pasta. Tip the flour onto a clean, dry work surface and make a well in the centre. Add the eggs to the well with the oil and salt. Gradually mix the liquid ingredients into the flour with your fingertips, adding more flour if the dough is too moist. Knead the dough until it is smooth and elastic. Gather it into a ball, wrap in cling film and leave to rest for 30 minutes to 1 hour.

Roll out the pasta dough very thinly, using a pasta machine if possible.

Alternatively use a rolling pin to roll out the dough until paper thickness. Cut into long fine strips and cook in boiling salted water for 30 seconds. Refresh in cold water and drain thoroughly. Add a few drops of olive oil, toss and set aside.

To prepare the vegetables, cut the carrots into fine strips, about 10 cm (5 inches) long. Repeat with the courgettes, discarding the seeds in the centre. Blanch the carrot strips in boiling water for 3 minutes; drain, refresh in cold water, drain and set aside.

To make the sauce, heat 25 g (1 oz) of the butter in a frying pan, add the shallots and sweat over a medium heat until translucent. Add the wine and fish stock and boil to reduce by half. Add the double cream and bring back to the boil. Dice the remaining butter and whisk into the sauce, a piece at a time. Strain and keep warm.

To cook the fish, season the salmon fillets with salt and pepper. Preheat a griddle or heavy-based pan and dry-fry the salmon over a high heat for 1½ minutes each side. Season with a little more pepper, to taste.

Meanwhile, finish the fettucine of vegetables. Melt the butter in a pan with about 45 ml (3 tbsp) water to form an emulsion. Poach the courgettes in the emulsion for 1 minute. Add the carrots and cooked tagliatelle; simmer for 1 minute, stirring to mix thoroughly. Drain and divide into 4 portions. Twist each portion of vegetables and pasta round a large fork or spoon to form a ball shape.

Add the lemon juice to the sauce to taste and check the seasoning. Place the salmon fillets on warmed serving plates and surround with the sauce. Add a ball of fettucine vegetables to each plate. Garnish with the sliced dates and tarragon sprigs.

ORANGE ALMOND TART WITH GINGER AND HONEY ICE CREAM

Pastry:
225 g (8 oz) plain flour
75 g (3 oz) icing sugar
125 g (4 oz) unsalted butter, diced
finely grated rind of 1 orange
1 egg, beaten

Tart Filling:
5 large firm oranges
15 ml (1 tbsp) Grand Marnier
30 ml (2 tbsp) icing sugar
125 g (4 oz) butter
75 g (3 oz) caster sugar
2 eggs (size 1)
150 g (5 oz) ground almonds
120 ml (4 fl oz) sieved orange marmalade

Ice Cream:
2 eggs, separated
25 g (1 oz) icing sugar
180 ml (6 fl oz) double cream
15 ml (1 tbsp) honey
2 pieces of preserved stem ginger in syrup, drained and sliced

To make the pastry, sift the flour and icing sugar into a bowl and rub in the butter until the mixture resembles breadcrumbs. Add the orange rind and egg. Mix with a round-bladed knife, then lightly knead the dough until smooth. Wrap in cling film and leave to rest in the refrigerator for 30 minutes.

To make the ice cream, whisk the egg yolks and icing sugar together in a bowl until pale. In another bowl, whip the cream until thick and combine it with the honey; add to the yolk and sugar mixture. Whisk the egg whites until stiff, then fold into the mixture with the ginger. Transfer to an ice-cream maker and freeze until firm.

Roll out the pastry on a lightly floured surface to about a 3 mm (⅛ inch)

thickness. Cut out 4 circles, large enough to line 4 individual flan tins, allowing some overhang. (Use a suitable plate or upturned bowl as a guide). Lightly grease and flour the flan tins, then fold the dough circles into them gently easing it into the corners and letting a little dough overhang. Line with greaseproof paper and fill with baking beans to ensure the sides are weighted as well as the base. Bake blind in a preheated oven at 180°C (350°F) mark 4 for 10 minutes. Remove the beans and paper and trim the edges of the pastry. Return to the oven for 10 minutes.

To prepare the tart filling, peel the oranges, removing all of the white pith. Cut the orange segments away from the membrane and place in a shallow dish. Squeeze any juice from the membranes over the segments and sprinkle with the Grand Marnier and icing sugar too. Cover and leave to macerate for 30 minutes.

Meanwhile, cream the butter and sugar together in a bowl, using an electric beater, until light and fluffy. Beat in the eggs, one at a time. Stir in the ground almonds and flour until evenly incorporated. Spread the almond mixture in the flan cases and bake in the oven for 20-25 minutes until golden. Allow to cool slightly.

Drain the orange segments, reserving 30 ml (2 tbsp) of the liquor. Place the marmalade and reserved liquor in a saucepan. Bring to the boil and reduce for 1-2 minutes. Brush this glaze onto the tarts, arrange the orange segments in circles on top and brush with more glaze.

Serve the tarts still slightly warm or cool, accompanied by the ice cream.

Note: If you do not have an ice-cream machine, freeze the ice cream in a suitable container, whisking periodically during freezing to break down the ice crystals, for an even-textured result.

THE SOUTH EAST

CLARE ASKAROFF • JOANNA CROSSLEY • ANN NEALE

PANEL OF JUDGES

Brian Turner • Ginny Elliot • Loyd Grossman

WINNER

CLARE ASKAROFF'S MENU

STARTER

Stuffed Pheasant Breast with Caramelised Calvados Apples

"Wonderful flavours" **Brian Turner**

MAIN COURSE

*Salmon Fillet on a bed of Courgette and Ginger with an Orange Butter Sauce
Parsnip and Potato Cakes*

"I loved the presentation of the salmon, and the colour and everything" **Ginny Elliot**

DESSERT

Melt-in-the-Mouth Meringue with a Red Berry Compote

"A fabulous pudding... it was delicious" **Loyd**

Clare Askaroff comes from Herstmonceux in East Sussex. Most of Clare's time is now taken up with her busy family, including her elder daughter Camilla who was the winner of Junior Masterchef 1994. Clare is an avid collector of all kinds of items – from old linen to honeypots, candlesticks to corkscrews – and she is a regular visitor to the local antique shops. Before starting her family, Clare was an illustrator specialising in plants and herbs, and she still likes to keep her hand in.

STUFFED PHEASANT BREAST WITH CARAMELISED CALVADOS APPLES

If possible, obtain hen pheasants for this recipe. Use the carcasses to make the game stock. You will also need 4 muslin squares, each 30 x 23 cm (12 x 9 inches), for cooking the pheasant breasts.

4 boneless, skinless pheasant breasts
600 ml (1 pint) game stock

Pâté:
1 Cox's apple
75 g (3 oz) unsalted butter
15 ml (1 tbsp) Calvados
1 slice smoked back bacon, cut into strips
25 g (1 oz) finely chopped onion
leaves from 3 thyme sprigs
125 g (4 oz) chicken livers, trimmed and
*   roughly chopped*
salt and freshly ground black pepper

Caramelised Apples:
2 Cox's apples
50 g (2 oz) butter
30-45 ml (2-3 tbsp) Calvados
salt and freshly ground black pepper
30-45 ml (2-3 tbsp) double cream

To Serve:
few chopped toasted hazelnuts (optional)
flat-leaved parsley sprigs

First make the pâté. Peel, core and slice the apple. Melt 25 g (1 oz) of the butter in a pan, add the apple with the Calvados and cook until soft; set aside. Meanwhile melt the remaining butter in a frying pan, add the bacon and onion and cook gently until softened. Add the thyme and chicken livers and cook for 1-2 minutes; do not overcook.

Place the apples and liver mixture in a food processor and process briefly to make a coarse paté. Season liberally with salt and pepper. Allow to cool slightly.

Carefully make a deep horizontal slit in each pheasant breast to form a pocket. Stuff with the paté, then wrap each one tightly in muslin and tie with string. Heat the stock in a wide shallow pan and season with salt and pepper. Add the parcels and poach for 7 minutes until just cooked. Remove the parcels from the pan and leave to rest (still wrapped) in a warm place.

Meanwhile, prepare the caramelised apples. Peel, core and slice the apples. Heat the butter in a pan and add the apples and 15 ml (1 tbsp) Calvados. Cook until the apples are golden and brown at the edges. Season liberally with salt. Remove the apples with a slotted spoon and keep warm. Deglaze the pan with the rest of the Calvados, then whisk in the cream. Season with salt and pepper to taste.

To serve, open up the parcels and slice each pheasant breast very carefully into 5-6 slices. Arrange in a semi-circle to one side of each warmed serving plate. Place a spoonful of caramelised apples on the other side. Reheat the sauce if necessary and drizzle over the meat. Sprinkle a few chopped toasted hazelnuts onto the apple and garnish with flat-leaved parsley.

Salmon Fillet on a bed of Courgette and Ginger with an Orange Butter Sauce

4 skinless salmon fillets, each about
   140 g (4½ oz)
4 courgettes, about 525 g (1¼ lb) total
   weight
salt and freshly ground black pepper
olive oil and butter, for frying
10 ml (2 tsp) grated fresh root ginger
30 ml (2 tbsp) chopped chives
30 ml (2 tbsp) chopped tarragon

Dressing:
juice of 1 lime, ie 22 ml (1½ tbsp)
60 ml (4 tbsp) sunflower oil
10 ml (2 tsp) caster sugar
5 ml (1 tsp) coarse-grain mustard
freshly ground black pepper, to taste

Sauce:
120 ml (4 fl oz) fish stock (see below)
juice of 1 very large orange, ie 120 ml
   (4 fl oz)
15 ml (1 tbsp) wine vinegar
3 egg yolks
225 g (8 oz) unsalted butter
rind of 1 orange, removed in thin strips
   with a zester

To Garnish:
12 cherry tomatoes, halved and grilled
few steamed asparagus tips
fried courgette skin (see note)

Coarsely grate the courgettes, place in a colander and sprinkle with salt. Leave to stand (over a plate to collect the degorged juices) for 2 hours.

Meanwhile, prepare the dressing. Put all of the ingredients into a screw-topped jar and shake well to combine; set aside. Prepare the garnish at this stage too.

For the sauce, put the fish stock and orange juice in a pan and boil to reduce by half. In a separate pan, bring the wine vinegar to the boil. Immediately pour onto the egg yolks, whisking constantly, preferably using a hand-held blender. Melt the butter in a pan, then very slowly add to the yolk mixture, whisking all the time; it will become very thick. Whisk in enough of the reduced stock and orange juice to give a smooth pouring consistency. Stir in the orange zest.

Season the salmon fillets liberally with salt and pepper. Brush with oil and cook under a preheated hot grill for 2-3 minutes each side. (Alternatively, fry in a little oil and butter for 1-2 minutes, then finish off under the grill for 1 minute).

Meanwhile, squeeze excess water from the courgettes, then toss with the ginger and steam for 1 minute to just heat through. Mix with the herbs and 30 ml (2 tbsp) of the dressing.

To serve, pile the courgette mixture onto warmed serving plates and surround with the sauce. Arrange the salmon on the courgette and top with the fried courgette skin. Garnish the plates with cherry tomatoes and asparagus tips. Serve accompanied by parsnip and potato cakes.

Note: To prepare this garnish, use a zester to remove strips of skin from 2 courgettes. Fry in sunflower oil until crisp; drain on kitchen paper.

Fish Stock: For this you will need about 1 kg (2 lb) washed fish bones and heads:

use the bones from the salmon, plus plaice or sole bones. Heat 25 g (1 oz) unsalted butter in a large pan. Add 1 leek, chopped; 1 onion, finely chopped; 1 carrot, diced; and 1 stick celery, diced. Sweat the vegetables until soft, then add the fish heads and bones and cook for 1-2 minutes. Add 300 ml (½ pint) dry white wine, bring to the boil and boil for 1-2 minutes. Add 1.2 litres (2 pints) cold water, a small bunch of parsley and 2 bay leaves. Return to the boil and boil for 2 minutes, then skim the surface. Simmer for 20 minutes only. Let cool a little, then strain through a sieve. Strain again through a muslin-lined sieve. Makes about 1.2 litres (2 pints).

PARSNIP AND POTATO CAKES

225 g (8 oz) parsnips
225 g (8 oz) floury potatoes (eg King Edward)
1 small clove garlic, crushed
15 g (½ oz) butter, plus extra if necessary
5 ml (1 tsp) dry mustard
salt and freshly ground black pepper
60 ml (4 tbsp) seasoned plain flour
2 eggs, beaten
3 slices wholemeal bread
30 ml (2 tbsp) sesame seeds
sunflower oil, for deep-frying (see note)

Peel the parsnips and potatoes, then cut into chunks. Cook in boiling salted water until soft.

Meanwhile cook the crushed garlic gently in the butter.

Drain the parsnips and potatoes. Mash until smooth, then beat in the garlic butter and mustard. Add a little more butter if necessary. Season well. Let cool, then chill the mixture for about 20 minutes.

Have ready 3 bowls: one containing the seasoned flour; one containing the beaten eggs. Process the bread to make breadcrumbs and mix with the sesame seeds in the third bowl.

Shape the parsnip and potato mixture into 10 small balls. Roll each ball first in the flour, then in the beaten egg, then finally in breadcrumbs. Place on a plate and chill until needed.

Just before serving, heat the oil for deep-frying. Deep-fry the parsnip and potato balls in batches until golden brown. Drain on kitchen paper and serve piping hot.

Note: For extra flavour, add 30 ml (2 tbsp) sesame oil to the oil for deep-frying.

MELT-IN-THE-MOUTH MERINGUE

5 egg whites
225 g (8 oz) caster sugar
5 ml (1 tsp) wine vinegar
5 ml (1 tsp) vanilla extract
10-15 ml (2-3 tsp) cornflour

To Assemble:

200 ml (7 fl oz) crème fraîche (not low-fat)
15 ml (1 tbsp) toasted flaked almonds
vanilla icing sugar (see right), for dusting

Caramel:

60 ml (4 tbsp) caster sugar

To Serve:

Red Berry Compote (see right)
4 mint sprigs

Line a 33 x 23 cm (13 x 9 inch) Swiss roll tin with non-stick baking parchment.

Whisk the egg whites in a bowl until very stiff. Whisk in the caster sugar 15 ml (1 tbsp) at a time, then whisk in the vinegar, vanilla extract and cornflour.

Spread the meringue evenly in the Swiss roll tin. Bake in a preheated oven at 180°C (350°F) mark 4 for 10 minutes. Leave in the tin to cool.

When cold, cut the meringue into eight 6 cm (2½ inch) squares. Grease a sheet of foil or a very clean baking sheet with oil. Place 4 meringue squares on the foil and top with the crème fraîche. Place another square of meringue on top at an angle. Sprinkle with a few toasted flaked almonds and dust with vanilla icing sugar.

Just before serving make the caramel. Dissolve the sugar in 120 ml (8 tbsp) water in a heavy-based pan over a low heat. Increase the heat and cook, without stirring, to a golden brown caramel. Drizzle the caramel over the top of the meringues, allowing it to run down the sides.

Dust each serving plate with vanilla icing sugar and carefully position a meringue on the plate. Place a generous spoonful of fruit compote alongside the meringue. Decorate with mint sprigs. Serve immediately.

Vanilla Icing Sugar: Bury a vanilla pod in a jar of icing sugar and leave for a few days to infuse. As you use it, top up the jar with more icing sugar.

RED BERRY COMPOTE

For this summer fruit compote, choose the fruits according to availability.

450 g (1 lb) mixed soft fruits, (eg raspberries, redcurrants, blackcurrants, strawberries, stoned cherries, blackberries)
15 ml (1 tbsp) concentrated blackcurrant Ribena
125 g (4 oz) caster sugar
15 ml (1 tbsp) potato flour (approximately)
icing sugar, for dusting

Put the fruit in a heavy-based pan and heat very gently for about 1 minute until the juices start to run. Drain the fruit very carefully so as not to damage it; transfer to a bowl and set aside. Measure the strained juice together with the Ribena. Add the caster sugar.

Return the juice to the pan and thicken with the potato flour: use 15 ml (1 tbsp) flour per 300 ml (½ pint) juice. Mix the flour with 30-45 ml (2-3 tbsp) water, stir into the juice and cook, stirring, for 1-2 minutes. Let cool slightly then pour over the fruit. Sift a little icing sugar over the surface to prevent a skin forming, then cover and chill in the refrigerator until needed. Serve with the Melt-in-the-Mouth Meringue.

THE SOUTH EAST

CLARE ASKAROFF • JOANNA CROSSLEY • ANN NEALE

PANEL OF JUDGES

Brian Turner • Ginny Elliot • Loyd Grossman

JOANNA CROSSLEY'S MENU

STARTER

*Mussels and Scallops in a Saffron Sauce
with Fresh Tagliatelle and Tomatoes*

"I thought that was delicious, excellent" **Ginny Elliot**

MAIN COURSE

Fillet of Lamb wrapped in Spinach and Prosciutto

Potato and Herb Layers

Mediterranean Vegetables

"The lamb was perfectly cooked. The Mediterranean vegetables were delicious" **Loyd**

DESSERT

Sticky Toffee Pudding Hearts

"The sticky pudding, for me, was one of the nicest, lightest,
I've had in a long time" **Brian Turner**

Joanna Crossley lives in Orpington, Kent. Joanna works for a company which manufactures essential medical equipment, and she frequently visits hospital special care units to instruct staff on the use of these products. To keep fit, Joanna takes to the water for some vigorous aquaerobics. At weekends she and her son Andrew often visit the animals at Godstone Farm.

Mussels and Scallops in a Saffron Sauce with Fresh Tagliatelle and Tomatoes

175-225 g (6-8 oz) mussels, cleaned
6-8 scallops, cleaned
2 plum tomatoes
25 g (1 oz) unsalted butter

Pasta Dough:
250 g (9 oz) plain flour
pinch of salt
2.5 ml (½ tsp) olive oil
2 eggs (size 2)
3 egg yolks (size 2)

Sauce:
10 ml (2 tsp) olive oil
½ small onion, finely chopped
1 clove garlic, finely chopped
200 ml (7 fl oz) white wine
1.25 ml (¼ tsp) saffron threads, crushed
75 ml (2 ½ fl oz) double cream

To Serve:
finely chopped basil

To make the pasta dough, put the flour, salt and olive oil into a food processor (fitted with a dough hook if you have one). Process for a few seconds, then add the eggs and egg yolks. Process until the dough comes together and forms a smooth ball. Wrap in cling film and leave to rest in the refrigerator for at least 30 minutes.

Slice off about a quarter of the dough; keep the rest wrapped so it does not dry out. Put the dough through a pasta machine on its thickest setting a few times, dusting with a little flour if it is too sticky. Proceed through the machine settings, gradually narrowing the setting each time until you reach No. 6. Fit the tagliatelle cutters and pass the pasta through. Hang the tagliatelle to dry. Repeat with the rest of the dough. (You will only need to use about half of this pasta; the rest can be frozen for future use.)

For the sauce, heat 10 ml (2 tsp) olive oil in a pan, add the onion and garlic and cook until softened. Add the white wine, bring to the boil, then add the saffron. Take off the heat and set aside for 20-30 minutes to allow the saffron to 'infuse'.

Put the tomatoes in a bowl, pour on boiling water and leave for 30 seconds. Remove with a slotted spoon and peel away the skins. Halve, deseed and chop the flesh into small pieces; set aside.

Reheat the wine, then add the mussels, cover with a tight-fitting lid and cook for 3-4 minutes until the shells have opened; take care to avoid overcooking them. Remove the mussels with a slotted spoon and set aside, discarding any that remain open. Strain the wine sauce through a muslin-lined sieve into a clean pan.

Slice each scallop horizontally into two or three rounds, depending on size. Heat the butter in a heavy-based pan, add the scallops and sear over a high heat for 30 seconds each side. Meanwhile add the cream to the wine sauce and simmer to reduce a little. Add the mussels and scallops and keep warm over a low heat. Add the tagliatelle to a large pan of boiling water. Cook for 1-2 minutes only, until *al dente* (tender but firm to the bite). Drain and add to the mussels and scallops. Toss lightly to mix, adding the chopped tomato. Serve at once, sprinkled with finely chopped basil.

FILLETS OF LAMB WRAPPED IN SPINACH AND PROSCIUTTO

2 loin of lamb fillets, each about 225 g (8 oz)
10 ml (2 tsp) olive oil
salt and freshly ground black pepper
8-10 large spinach leaves, stalks removed
5 ml (1 tsp) French mustard
5 ml (1 tsp) Dijon mustard
2.5 ml (½ tsp) wholegrain mustard
2.5 ml (½ tsp) chopped dill
4-6 slices prosciutto or Parma ham
2-3 shallots, finely chopped
1 clove garlic, finely chopped
200 ml (7 fl oz) rosé wine
250 ml (8 fl oz) veal or lamb stock
2.5 ml (½ tsp) tomato purée

Heat the olive oil in a heavy-based pan, add the lamb fillets and seal on all sides over a high heat. Season with salt and pepper and set aside. (Don't rinse the pan).

Plunge the spinach leaves into a pan of boiling water, then remove immediately so as not to overcook them. Lay them out on a clean tea-towel to drain. Spread out, overlapping the leaves slightly to form two 'sheets' of spinach.

Mix the mustards together with the dill. Spread all but 2.5 ml (½ tsp) evenly on both sheets of spinach.

Place a lamb fillet on each spinach sheet and wrap the spinach around the lamb to enclose completely. Lay out the prosciutto slices, overlapping them slightly to form two 'sheets'. Place the lamb fillets on top and fold the prosciutto around each fillet to enclose. The prosciutto should adhere to itself and hold together, but if at all concerned, tie at intervals with cotton string to hold it in place. (Wrap in cling film and left to rest in a cool place until ready to cook.)

Roast the lamb in a preheated oven at 220°C (425°F) mark 7 for 15-20 minutes, depending on how you like your lamb. Meanwhile make the gravy. Reheat the oil remaining in the pan used to seal the lamb, add the shallots and garlic and cook until softened. Deglaze with the rosé wine, stirring to scrape up the sediment. Simmer to reduce by one third then add the stock and reduce again by about a third.

Strain the sauce through a conical sieve or pass through a mouli to purée the shallot and garlic. Return to the pan, add the tomato purée and if necessary, reduce to the desired consistency. Add a little of the reserved mustard mixture to taste.

Cover the lamb lightly with foil and let rest for at least 5 minutes.

To serve, slice each lamb fillet into 3 or 4 medallions, depending on size. Arrange on warmed plates and serve with the sauce and accompaniments.

POTATO AND HERB LAYERS

675 g (1½ lb) potatoes
butter, for greasing
200 ml (7 fl oz) double cream
90 ml (3 fl oz) milk
salt and freshly ground black pepper
30 ml (2 tbsp) chopped mixed herbs
   (parsley, thyme, chives and tarragon)

Butter 4 individual gratin dishes. Slice the potatoes finely, using a mandolin. Mix the cream and milk together. Layer the potatoes in the gratin dishes, seasoning each layer and sprinkling with chopped herbs, to form 2 or 3 potato layers; arrange the top layer in a 'pattern' for effect. Pour on the cream and milk mixture and sprinkle with pepper. Place on a baking sheet and bake in a preheated oven at 190°C (375°F) mark 5 for 40-45 minutes until crisp and browned on top and cooked through. Alternatively, microwave on HIGH for 4 minutes, then bake in the oven for a further 20 minutes. Serve in the gratin dishes or lift onto warmed serving plates.

MEDITERRANEAN VEGETABLES

1 aubergine
sea salt and freshly ground black pepper
3 courgettes
1 onion
1 green pepper, cored and deseeded
1 red pepper, cored and deseeded
1 yellow pepper, cored and deseeded
4 plum tomatoes
olive oil, for frying
1 clove garlic, chopped

Cut the aubergine into 5 mm (¼ inch) slices and layer in a colander, sprinkling with salt. Place a small plate on top and weight down. Leave to drain.

Slice the remaining vegetables to about the same thickness as the aubergine. Heat a little olive oil in a heavy-based frying pan and sauté the onion and garlic until almost soft; remove from the pan and set aside.

Rinse the aubergine slices under cold running water and pat dry. Heat a little more olive oil in the pan, add the aubergines and fry on both sides until golden brown.

Either blanch the courgettes and peppers in boiling water, or microwave on HIGH for 1-2 minutes until softened. Position four 7.5 cm (3 inch) metal ring moulds on a baking tray. Layer the vegetables in the moulds, starting with the aubergine slices and finishing with the tomato slices. Drizzle a generous 5 ml (1 tsp) olive oil on top of each one. Bake in a preheated oven at 190°C (375°F) mark 5 for about 25 minutes. Lift onto warmed serving plates, using a fish slice, and remove the metal rings. Serve at once.

STICKY TOFFEE PUDDING HEARTS

175 g (6 oz) dates, stoned and chopped
5 ml (1 tsp) bicarbonate of soda
50 g (2 oz) unsalted butter
175 g (6 oz) caster sugar
2 eggs
175 g (6 oz) self-raising flour
5 ml (1 tsp) vanilla essence
icing sugar, for dusting

Sauce:
300 ml (½ pint) double cream
50 g (2 oz) demerara sugar
10 ml (2 tsp) black treacle

Put the dates in a saucepan and pour on 300 ml (½ pint) boiling water. Simmer for about 4 minutes until the dates are soft, then add the bicarbonate of soda.

Meanwhile cream the butter and sugar together in a bowl. Add the eggs, one at a time, beating well. Add the dates with their liquid, the flour and vanilla essence; mix lightly until evenly blended. Pour into a greased 30 x 18 cm (12 x 7 inch) Swiss roll tin.

Bake in a preheated oven at 180°C (350°F) mark 4 for about 30 minutes or until springy to the touch and lightly browned. Turn onto a wire rack and let cool for 5 minutes.

Meanwhile put the sauce ingredients in a saucepan and heat through, stirring; keep warm.

Turn the sponge onto a board and cut out 4 large hearts using a suitable heart-shaped cutter. Sprinkle with icing sugar and, using a hot skewer, 'score' a criss-cross pattern on the surface. Pour the hot sauce on to 4 warmed serving plates and position the hearts on top. Serve at once.

THE SOUTH EAST

CLARE ASKAROFF • JOANNA CROSSLEY • ANN NEALE

PANEL OF JUDGES

Brian Turner • Ginny Elliot • Loyd Grossman

ANN NEALE'S MENU

STARTER

Marrow and Cumin Soup

"The texture was good, and the flavours were nice" **Brian Turner**

MAIN COURSE

Beef and Mushroom Pudding

Buttered Spinach

Seasonal Vegetables

"The taste and consistency of the pastry were wonderful.
The beef was tremendous, that was a real powerhouse" **Brian Turner**

DESSERT

Bramble Mousse with Bramble Sauce, served with Almond Biscuits

"I thought the texture of that mousse was sensational" **Brian Turner**

Ann Neale comes from East Grinstead in West Sussex. Ann works at Sackville School as a technician in the Home Economics department. In her spare time Ann is a keen wine-maker. She also has an impressive collection of ornamental frogs – some 500 in all – which live all over her home!

MARROW AND CUMIN SOUP

2 medium potatoes, about 225 g (8 oz)
total weight
salt and freshly ground black pepper
1 small marrow, or 450 g (1 lb) courgettes
10 ml (2 tsp) cumin seeds
150 ml (¼ pint) soured cream
chopped parsley, for sprinkling

Peel the potatoes, place in a saucepan and cover with plenty of salted water.

Peel and core the marrow or courgettes, cut into pieces and put into a steamer. Tie the cumin seeds in a square of muslin and add to the marrow.

Place the steamer on top of the saucepan of potatoes. Bring to the boil and simmer for about 20 minutes until the potatoes are tender and the marrow is softened. Discard the cumin.

Put the marrow or courgettes and potatoes in a blender or food processor with 600 ml (1 pint) of the cooking water. Work until smooth, then return to the pan. Reheat gently. Divide between warmed soup bowls and top each serving with a generous swirl of soured cream and a sprinkling of chopped parsley. Serve at once.

BEEF AND MUSHROOM PUDDING

Beef Stock:
6 beef bones
50 g (2 oz) butter
1 large onion, chopped
1 carrot
1 stick celery
bouquet garni (rosemary, sage and thyme
sprigs and a bay leaf tied in muslin)
salt and freshly ground black pepper

Puddings:
450 g (1 lb) flank of beef
175 g (6 oz) beef suet
175 g (6 oz) chestnut mushrooms
350 g (12 oz) self-raising flour

Sauce:
125 g (4 oz) oyster or shiitake mushrooms
150 ml (¼ pint) red wine

To make the beef stock, melt the butter in a pressure cooker, add the beef bones and onion and fry, stirring, until browned. Add the carrot and celery. Pour in 1.5 litres (2½ pints) water and add the bouquet garni and seasoning. Bring to pressure and cook for 45 minutes. Reduce the pressure slowly. Strain the stock and allow to cool. When cold, remove the fat from the surface.

To make the puddings, grate the suet and refrigerate. Cut the meat into 1 cm (½ inch) cubes and put into the pressure cooker with the beef stock. Bring to pressure and cook for 15 minutes. Cool quickly under cold running water. Strain off the stock and refrigerate the stock and meat separately. When cold, skim the fat off the surface of the stock.

Put a large saucepan of water on to boil for the puddings. Slice the chestnut mushrooms and mix with the meat.

To make the suetcrust pastry, sift the flour with a pinch of salt into a bowl. Add the grated suet and mix with a round-bladed knife, adding enough water to yield a firm, not sticky dough. Cover and refrigerate for 15 minutes.

Divide the dough into 4 equal pieces and roll each portion out to a 15 cm (6 inch) round. Cut a quarter wedge out of each round and reserve for the top. Butter 4 individual 150 ml (¼ pint) pudding moulds well and line with the pastry. Fill with the beef and mushroom mixture and add 15 ml (1 tbsp) stock to each. Shape the reserved pastry into rounds to fit the tops and place in position. Cover with a round of buttered greaseproof paper and a square of muslin. Secure with string around the rim. Put the puddings into the steamer and cook for about 45 minutes until the pastry is risen and light.

Meanwhile, pour the stock into a saucepan. Season and add the chopped oyster or shiitake mushrooms together with the wine. Simmer to reduce to a sauce consistency. Check the seasoning.

Turn out the pudding on to warmed individual plates, and surround with the sauce. Serve with the buttered spinach and seasonal vegetables.

Note: If you do not have a pressure cooker you will need to allow longer for cooking the stock and meat. Simmer the stock in a saucepan for 1½ hours. Similarly allow 30 minutes for cooking the meat in the stock.

BUTTERED SPINACH

225 g (8 oz) young spinach leaves
25 g (1 oz) butter

Wash the spinach and place in a pan with just the water clinging to the leaves after washing. Cover and cook over a moderate heat for about 30 seconds.

Butter 4 ramekin dishes and fill with the spinach, pressing it down firmly. Cover each ramekin with a round of well-buttered greaseproof paper and place in a steamer. Steam for about 15 minutes until tender. Turn on to a hot serving plate and serve immediately.

BRAMBLE MOUSSE WITH BRAMBLE SAUCE

675 g (1½ lb) wild blackberries
1 sachet powdered gelatine
150 ml (¼ pint) whipping cream
50 g (2 oz) icing sugar, sifted
2 egg whites (size 1)

Sauce:
120 ml (8 tbsp) reserved blackberry purée
  (see recipe)
25 g (1 oz) icing sugar, sifted

To Decorate:
borage or other edible flowers
mint leaves

Set aside a few blackberries for decoration. Put the rest into a blender or food processor and work until smooth. Set aside about 120 ml (8 tbsp) blackberry purée for the sauce.

Sprinkle the gelatine over 45 ml (3 tbsp) cold water in a small bowl and leave to soak for 2-3 minutes. Stand the bowl over a pan of simmering water until dissolved.

Lightly whip the cream. Stir the icing sugar into the blackberry purée with the dissolved gelatine, then fold in the cream. Whisk the egg whites until stiff and gently fold in the blackberry mousse mixture.

Divide the mousse between four 150 ml (¼ pint) ramekins or other individual moulds. Chill in the refrigerator for at least 1 hour until set.

To serve, turn each mousse out on to a dessert plate. For the sauce, stir the icing sugar into the reserved blackberry purée and spoon around the mousse. Decorate with borage or other edible flowers, mint leaves and the reserved blackberries. Serve accompanied by the almond biscuits.

ALMOND BISCUITS

50 g (2 oz) butter
25 g (1 oz) caster sugar
50 g (2 oz) plain flour, sifted
50 g (2 oz) ground almonds
5 drops of almond essence
icing sugar, for dusting

Cream the butter and sugar together in a bowl until smooth. Add the flour, ground almonds and almond essence. Mix together, using a round-bladed knife, until evenly incorporated. Knead lightly.

Roll out the dough on a lightly floured surface to a 5 mm (¼ inch) thickness. Cut into shapes, using a pastry cutter and transfer to a baking sheet lined with non-stick baking parchment. Prick all over with a fork. Bake in a preheated oven at 180°C (350°F) mark 4 for 10-12 minutes until golden brown but not firm.

Leave to cool on the paper for 1 minute to firm up slightly, then carefully lift the biscuits on to a wire rack. Leave to cool, then dust with icing sugar. Serve with the bramble mousse.

———THE SOUTH WEST & WALES———

GARETH RICHARDS • ELIZABETH TRUSCOTT • JOHN WOODWARD

PANEL OF JUDGES

David Nicholls • Ian McCaskill • Loyd Grossman

WINNER

GARETH RICHARDS' MENU

STARTER

Trellis of Sole and Salmon,
served with Chive and Cream Sauce

"It was absolutely marvellous – you could taste both fishes so clearly, and they both went so well with the sauce" **Ian McCaskill**

MAIN COURSE

Rosette of Welsh Lamb with Pistou Sauce

Potato Rösti, Baby Vegetables and Julienne of Leeks

"I thought that the lamb with pistou was absolutely fabulous" **Loyd**

DESSERT

Iced Caramelised Hazelnut Mousse with Raspberries and Port Coulis

"Today it's a dessert to die for, it was wonderful" **David Nicholls**

Gareth Richards, from Lampeter in Dyfed, works as an assistant in the dining hall at Lampeter University. Gareth also helps regularly on the family farm. Gareth has won many prizes for his floral art, and gives frequent demonstrations – in Welsh as well as English – to Women's Institute groups throughout the valleys.

TRELLIS OF SALMON AND SOLE, SERVED WITH CHIVE AND CREAM SAUCE

225 g (8 oz) salmon fillet
225 g (8 oz) sole fillet
150 ml (¼ pint) white wine
185 ml (6 fl oz) Noilly Prat
125 g (4 oz) chilled butter, diced
250 ml (8 fl oz) double cream
30 ml (2 tbsp) snipped chives, or to taste

To Garnish:
chives

Cut both the salmon and sole into finger-thick pieces; you will need 12 strips of each fish. Lay 3 strips of salmon on a board and weave 3 strips of sole through these. Repeat this process with the other strips to make 4 trellis. Place in a shallow baking tin and pour in the wine. Cover with foil and cook in a preheated oven at 200°C (400°F) mark 6 for 10-15 minutes.

Meanwhile make the sauce. Simmer the Noilly Prat until it has reduced by half. Let cool slightly, then whisk in the butter a little at a time. Whisk the cream into the sauce, until thick and glossy. Add the snipped chives to taste. Heat through gently before serving.

To serve, pour some of the sauce on to each warmed serving plate and position the salmon and sole trellis on top. Garnish with chives.

ROSETTE OF WELSH LAMB WITH PISTOU SAUCE

2 fillets of Welsh lamb, each about
 225-300 g (8-10 oz)
25 g (1 oz) butter
15 ml (1 tbsp) olive oil
salt and freshly ground black pepper

Pistou Sauce:
handful of basil leaves
12 stems of parsley
30 ml (2 tbsp) pine nuts
1 clove garlic
300 ml (½ pint) well-flavoured homemade lamb stock
125 g (4 oz) butter

Vegetables:
4 carrots
½ swede
1 leek
unsalted butter, for cooking
2 potatoes
5 ml (1 tsp) freshly grated nutmeg

To Garnish:
basil sprigs

To make the pistou sauce, blanch the herbs in boiling water for 15 seconds, then refresh in iced water. Drain and chop finely. Press through a sieve. Toast the pine nuts, then grind with the garlic. Place the stock, butter, herbs and garlic mixture in a saucepan. Bring to the boil and reduce by half; keep warm.

To prepare the vegetables, 'turn' the carrots and swede by cutting into classic barrel shapes of uniform size. Cook in boiling salted water until tender; drain and keep warm. Cut the leek into julienne strips. Sweat the leek in a pan with a knob of butter until tender.

To prepare the potato rösti, grate the potatoes and mix with the nutmeg and seasoning. Melt 40 g (1½ oz) butter in a heavy-based frying pan. Set four 7.5 cm (3 inch) metal rings in the pan. Divide the potato mixture evenly between the rings, pressing well down. Cook over a moderate heat for about 5 minutes until the underside is crisp and golden brown. Turn and cook the other side until crispy. Drain on kitchen paper.

Season the lamb fillets with salt and pepper. Heat the butter and olive oil in a heavy-based frying pan, add the lamb fillets and fry, turning frequently, for 5-6 minutes depending on thickness; they should still be pink inside. Remove from the pan, cover and leave to rest in a warm place for 5 minutes.

To serve, cut the lamb into noisettes. Position a rösti on each serving plate and top with leek julienne. Arrange the noisettes on top. Surround with the pistou sauce and vegetables. Garnish with basil.

ICED CARAMELISED HAZELNUT MOUSSE WITH RASPBERRIES AND PORT COULIS

25 g (1 oz) caster sugar
50 g (2 oz) hazelnuts, toasted
1 egg white
75 g (3 oz) icing sugar
120 ml (4 fl oz) double cream

Raspberry and Port Coulis:
225 g (8 oz) raspberries
45 ml (3 tbsp) port
25 g (1 oz) icing sugar

Coupelles:
50 g (2 oz) caster sugar
25 g (1 oz) plain flour
25 g (1 oz) butter, melted
1 egg white, lightly beaten

To Decorate:
raspberries
mint sprigs
icing sugar, for dusting

Put the caster sugar in a heavy-based pan and heat gently until melted. Continue cooking over a medium-low heat to a golden brown caramel. Carefully stir in the toasted hazelnuts and immediately pour onto an oiled marble slab or baking tray. Leave to cool until set, then grind coarsely.

Whisk the egg white until stiff peaks form, then gradually whisk in the icing sugar. In another bowl, whip the cream until soft peaks form. Fold the cream and hazelnut praline into the meringue, until evenly incorporated. Divide between 4 ramekin dishes and freeze for 1½ hours.

Meanwhile make the coulis. Purée the raspberries in a blender or food processor with the port and icing sugar. Pass through a sieve to remove the pips.

To make the coupelles, mix the sugar and flour together in a bowl. Stir in the melted butter, then fold in the egg white. Put 4 tablespoons of the mixture well apart on baking sheets lined with non-stick baking parchment. Spread out to form 4 thin circles and bake in a preheated oven at 180°C (350°F) mark 4 for 10 minutes. Leave for a moment or two, then mould each round over an orange to form a coupelle.

To serve, unmould the iced mousses onto individual serving plates. Surround with the raspberry and port coulis. Position a coupelle on each plate and fill with some raspberries. Decorate with mint and dust with icing sugar to serve.

——THE SOUTH WEST & WALES——

GARETH RICHARDS • ELIZABETH TRUSCOTT • JOHN WOODWARD

PANEL OF JUDGES

David Nicholls • Ian McCaskill • Loyd Grossman

ELIZABETH TRUSCOTT'S MENU

STARTER

*Sauté of Mixed Mushrooms
with Deep-fried Noodles*

"Great noodles" **David Nicholls**

MAIN COURSE

*Fillet of Dover Sole with a Fish Mousseline,
Fish Puffs and a Watercress Sauce*

Medley of Green Vegetables with a Dill Dressing

"I enjoy those sensitive delicate flavours" **Ian McCaskill**

DESSERT

*Pink Grapefruit Ice Cream in a Tuile Basket
with Citrus Fruits in a Honey Scented Dressing*

"Amazing. A great ice cream" **Loyd**

L iz Truscott comes from Bridport in West Dorset. Liz retired from full-time teaching a couple of years ago, but still plays an important part in helping the children with special needs at Beaminster Comprehensive. Her husband, Andy, is head of Design and Technology at the same school. Together they enjoy collecting and restoring antique furniture. Both are also boating enthusiasts, and Liz's claim to fame is that she was the first lady Commodore of the Lyme Regis Sailing Club.

SAUTÉ OF MIXED MUSHROOMS WITH DEEP-FRIED NOODLES

These quantities are really sufficient to serve 6 as a starter, or 4 as a main course if you prefer.

Noodles:
125 g (4 oz) strong plain flour
1.25 ml (¼ tsp) freshly grated nutmeg
1 egg (size 3), plus 1 egg yolk
salt and freshly ground black pepper
oil for deep-frying

Mushroom Sauté:
675 g (1½ lb) mixed mushrooms, (eg oyster, shiitake, chestnut, button)
10 ml (2 tsp) olive oil
25 g (1 oz) unsalted butter
4 shallots, chopped
15 ml (1 tbsp) amaretto di Saronno liqueur
150 ml (¼ pint) chicken stock
15 ml (1 tbsp) chopped parsley
15 ml (1 tbsp) chopped chervil

To make the pasta, sift the flour and nutmeg into a bowl. Make a well in the centre and add the egg, egg yolk, salt and pepper. Using your hand, draw the flour slowly into the centre mixing it with the egg as you do so. Knead the dough until smooth, wrap in cling film and leave to rest in the refrigerator for 30 minutes.

Roll the dough out very thinly, using a pasta machine if you have one, then cut into short noodles. Bring a large saucepan of water to the boil. Plunge the noodles into the pan and cook for 1 minute. Drain, then refresh in a bowl of cold water to cool. Drain and pat dry with kitchen paper.

To prepare the sauté, trim the stalks from the mushrooms. Put the stalks in a saucepan with 150 ml (¼ pint) water. Bring to the boil and simmer for 5 minutes, then strain the liquid and set aside for the mushroom stock. Discard the stalks.

Heat the oil and half of the butter in a large frying pan and sauté the mushrooms for 1 minute. Add the shallots and sauté for a further 1 minute.

Add the liqueur, with the reserved mushroom stock, and cook until the liquid is reduced by half. Add the chicken stock and cook until the liquid is again reduced by half.

Meanwhile, heat the oil for deep-frying in a large pan. When hot, deep-fry the noodles in batches for about 30 seconds until crisp and golden. Drain on kitchen paper.

Add the remaining butter and chopped herbs to the mushrooms. Season with salt and pepper to taste. Add the fried noodles and toss to mix. Serve immediately.

Note: If preferred, serve the mushrooms and noodles, accompanied by a salad of rocket or lamb's lettuce tossed in a little balsamic vinaigrette dressing.

FILLET OF DOVER SOLE WITH A FISH MOUSSELINE, FISH PUFFS AND A WATERCRESS SAUCE

If possible, get your fishmonger to bone the fish for you, remembering to ask for the bones which you will need for the stock.

2 Dover soles, each about 450 g (1 lb), skinned and filleted into 4 pieces

Fish Stock:
bones and white skin from the sole
15 g (½ oz) unsalted butter
1 small onion, chopped
50 ml (2 fl oz) dry white wine
bouquet garni (parsley, bay leaf, tarragon, fennel, chervil, white of leek, blade of mace)
1 shallot, finely chopped
3 thick lemon slices

Mousseline:
225 g (8 oz) whiting, filleted and skinned
1 egg white (size 3)
120 ml (4 fl oz) double cream
22 ml (1½ tbsp) chopped mixed herbs (parsley, tarragon, chervil)
salt and freshly ground black pepper

Pastry Fish:
150 g (5 oz) fresh puff pastry
egg yolk, to glaze

Watercress Sauce:
120 ml (4 fl oz) dry white wine
150 ml (¼ pint) double cream
1 bunch of watercress, stalks removed
15 ml (1 tbsp) cornflour

To Garnish:
tomato pieces
dill sprigs

To make the fish stock, melt the butter in a large saucepan, add the chopped onion and cook over a low heat for 2 minutes until soft but not coloured. Add the fish bones and cook for a further 2 minutes. Add the fish skin, 900 ml (1½ pints) water, the wine and bouquet garni. Bring to the boil, reduce the heat and simmer, uncovered, for 20 minutes.

To prepare the mousseline, place the whiting and egg white in a food processor and blend for 2-3 minutes. Press through a sieve into a bowl set over a bowl of ice. Gradually fold the cream into the mixture. Stir in the chopped herbs and season well. Put the mixture into a piping bag fitted with a large plain nozzle.

Place each sole fillet on a board, boned-side uppermost. Pipe some of the mousseline across the centre of each fillet. Gently roll up and secure each one with a wooden cocktail stick. Place in a greased roasting tin with the shallot and lemon slices. Pour in enough fish stock to cover the base of the tin. Cover the tin with greased greaseproof paper and set aside in a cool place.

To make the pastry fish, roll out the pastry on a lightly floured surface to a rectangle. On the lower half of the pastry, pipe 8 small portions of mousseline. Fold over the top half of the pastry and press gently together around the mousseline. Cut out 8 fish shapes (see note), making sure the filling is in the centre of each fish. Place on a baking sheet, brush with beaten egg yolk to glaze and sprinkle with salt crystals. Bake in a preheated oven at 200°C (400°F) mark 6 for 8-10 minutes until golden.

Cook the fish in the oven at the same temperature for 15 minutes.

For the watercress sauce, put 300 ml (½ pint) of the remaining fish stock and the wine in a pan. Bring to the boil and boil steadily until reduced by half. Stir in the cream and cook for 1 minute. Place the sauce and the watercress leaves in a blender or food processor and blend for 1 minute. Return the sauce to the pan. Mix the cornflour to a paste with 10 ml (2 tsp) cold water. Stir into the sauce and cook, stirring, until thickened and smooth.

To serve, remove the cocktail sticks from the sole. Serve on a pool of watercress sauce with the fish pastries. Garnish with tomato and dill.

Note: You may find it easier to use a template, cut from paper or card, as a guide when shaping the pastry fish.

MEDLEY OF GREEN VEGETABLES WITH A DILL DRESSING

125 g (4 oz) fine green beans
125 g (4 oz) sugar snap peas or mangetouts
125 g (4 oz) courgettes
125 g (4 oz) broccoli florets
salt
15 g (½ oz) slightly salted butter
10 ml (2 tsp) lemon juice
freshly ground mixed peppercorns
30 ml (2 tbsp) chopped fresh dill, or 2.5 ml (½ tsp) dried

Trim the beans and sugar snap peas. Trim the courgettes and thinly slice lengthwise to form fine ribbons, 1.5 cm (⅝ inch) wide. Divide the broccoli into small even-sized florets.

Cook the broccoli in a large pan of boiling salted water for 1 minute. Add the beans and sugar snap peas and cook for 2 minutes. Add the courgette ribbons and, as soon as the water returns to the boil, remove the pan from the heat. Drain the vegetables in a colander and refresh with cold water.

Melt the butter in a large frying pan over a moderate heat until sizzling. Add the vegetables and cook, shaking the pan constantly, for 1 minute. Add the lemon juice and freshly ground peppercorns to taste. Stir in the dill and serve at once.

Pink Grapefruit Ice Cream and Citrus Fruits in a Honey Dressing

Ice Cream:
finely grated rind and juice of 2 pink grapefruit
juice of 1 orange
juice of 1 lemon
75 g (3 oz) caster sugar
1 egg white (size 3)
150 ml (¼ pint) double cream

Citrus Fruits:
1 pink grapefruit
1 orange
1 yellow grapefruit or 1 ugli fruit

Dressing:
3 green cardamom pods, seeds only
45 ml (3 tbsp) clear honey
15 ml (1 tbsp) rose water

To Serve:
4 Tuile Baskets (see right)
lemon balm or mint sprigs, to decorate

To make the ice cream, put the grapefruit rind in a saucepan with the grapefruit, orange and lemon juices, and the sugar. Heat gently until the sugar is dissolved, then bring to the boil and simmer for 5 minutes until a light syrup is obtained.

Lightly whisk the egg white and gradually add it to the hot syrup, whisking all the time. Leave until cold. Stir in the cream and transfer to an ice-cream maker. Churn for approximately 20 minutes until frozen (see note).

To prepare the citrus fruits, peel, using a sharp knife, to remove all peel and white pith. Cut out the segments, free from the membranes; place in a bowl.

For the dressing, crush the cardamom seeds to a powder, then place in a small pan with the honey and rose water. Stir together over a moderate heat for 2 minutes. Set aside to cool.

To serve, place one scoop of ice cream in each tuile basket and arrange the citrus fruit segments in a fan alongside. Pour the dressing over the fruit and garnish with sprigs of lemon balm or mint.

Note: If you do not have an ice-cream maker, freeze the ice cream in a shallow container, whisking 2-3 times during freezing to break down the ice crystals and ensure an even-textured result.

Tuile Baskets

50 g (2 oz) butter, softened
50 g (2 oz) icing sugar, sifted
1 egg white (size 2)
45 g (1½ oz) plain flour, sifted
finely grated rind of ½ lemon

Cream the butter and icing sugar together in a bowl, then beat in the egg white, a little at a time. Fold in the flour and grated lemon rind. Cover and place in the refrigerator for at least 30 minutes.

Line 2 baking sheets with non-stick baking parchment. Draw on four or five 12 cm (5 inch) circles, using a saucer as a guide. Invert the paper.

Spread a thin layer of tuile mixture over each drawn circle. Bake in a preheated oven at 180°C (350°F) mark 4 for about 4 minutes until pale golden brown; do not allow the edges to become too crisp.

Carefully remove the biscuits with a palette knife and place each one over a small upturned ramekin dish. Press gently into shape.

Note: It's a good idea to make an extra tuile to allow for a breakage. Once cooked these tuiles do not keep well. However you can prepare the mixture in advance and store it in the refrigerator for several days.

——THE SOUTH WEST & WALES——

GARETH RICHARDS • ELIZABETH TRUSCOTT • JOHN WOODWARD

PANEL OF JUDGES

David Nicholls • Ian McCaskill • Loyd Grossman

JOHN WOODWARD'S MENU

STARTER

Salmon and Haddock Fish Cakes,
served with Gherkin Mayonnaise

"The fish cakes with the mayonnaise... the combination –
magic" **David Nicholls**

MAIN COURSE

Calves Kidney with Mustard Sauce

Bubble and Squeak

Hot Grated Beetroot

Glazed Carrots

"The kidneys with mustard sauce were unbeatable" **Ian McCaskill**

DESSERT

Chilled Semolina Pudding,
served with Raspberry and Mango Sauces

"I love semolina, so I was thrilled to have that" **Loyd**

———

John Woodward lives in Chard, Somerset. John is an organic farmer at the Magdalen Farm which is owned by a charitable trust and run by a like-minded group of enthusiasts. They hope soon to market the products of the farm's most recent venture – cheese-making. When they get time to relax, the group turn their hand and voices to some impressive musical entertainment.

SALMON AND HADDOCK FISH CAKES

Serve these tasty fish cakes with a home-made mayonnaise, spiked with chopped gherkins.

225 g (8 oz) salmon fillet
225 g (8 oz) haddock fillet
225 g (8 oz) potato (uncooked), peeled and
  diced
2 eggs
1 thick slice of white bread, crusts removed
90 ml (3 fl oz) single cream
salt and freshly ground black pepper
paprika
freshly grated nutmeg
30 ml (2 tbsp) oil
25 g (1 oz) unsalted butter

To Serve:
salad leaves
mayonnaise (see above)

Put the fish, potato, eggs and bread in a blender or food processor and work to a purée, adding the cream at the last moment. Pass through a fine sieve into a bowl and season with salt, pepper, a pinch or two of paprika and some freshly grated nutmeg.

Shape the mixture into small cakes, using two teaspoons. Heat the oil and butter in a frying pan, add the fish cakes and fry over a moderate heat, turning once until golden on both sides. Lower the heat and cook for a few minutes longer. Drain on kitchen paper.

Serve hot, on a bed of salad leaves, accompanied by mayonnaise flavoured with chopped pickled gherkins.

CALVES KIDNEY WITH MUSTARD SAUCE

900 g (2 lb) calves kidneys
salt and freshly ground black pepper
45 ml (3 tbsp) olive oil
50 g (2 oz) butter
1 shallot, chopped
225 g (8 oz) mushrooms, sliced
45 ml (3 tbsp) brandy
90 ml (6 tbsp) soured cream
45 ml (3 tbsp) wholegrain mustard
150 ml (¼ pint) lamb or veal stock
chopped parsley, to garnish

Remove any membrane from the kidneys and cut out the fatty core. Season with salt and pepper. Heat the olive oil and half of the butter in a heavy-based frying pan. Add the kidneys and sauté until they are browned all over. Reduce the heat and cook for about 10 minutes; they should still be pink in the middle. Keep warm.

Wipe the pan clean, then add the remaining butter and heat until melted. Add the shallot and cook until softened. Add the mushrooms, and cook, stirring, until they have absorbed all the moisture. Add the brandy and set alight. When the flames have died down, stir in the soured cream, mustard and stock. Let bubble until the sauce is reduced to the desired consistency.

Drain any juices from the warm kidneys, then slice. Arrange the sliced kidneys on warmed serving plates and spoon over the sauce. Sprinkle with chopped parsley and serve with the accompaniments.

BUBBLE AND SQUEAK

900 g (2 lb) potatoes
250 ml (8 fl oz) milk
225 g (8 oz) bacon, derinded and diced
8 spring onions, chopped
225 g (8 oz) Brussels sprouts
salt and freshly ground black pepper
7.5 ml (1½ tsp) flour
30 ml (2 tbsp) goose, duck or bacon fat, for
  frying

Peel the potatoes and cook in boiling salted water until tender. Drain thoroughly and dry well, then mash smoothly. Heat the milk and stir into the potato.

Fry the bacon in a heavy-based pan, without additional fat, until crispy. Remove with a slotted spoon and set aside; sauté the spring onions in the fat remaining in the pan until softened. Par-cook the Brussels sprouts in boiling salted water; they should still be slightly crunchy. Chop the sprouts and add them to the potato with the spring onions and bacon. Season well.

Shape the mixture into small cakes and coat with the flour, shaking off excess. Heat the fat in a frying pan and fry the vegetables cakes until brown and crispy on both sides. Serve piping hot.

CHILLED SEMOLINA PUDDING WITH RASPBERRY AND MANGO SAUCES

450 ml (¾ pint) single cream
15 ml (1 tbsp) caster sugar
finely grated rind of 1 lemon
finely grated rind of 1 orange
finely grated rind of 1 lime
25 g (1 oz) semolina
1 gelatine leaf
4 egg yolks, beaten
300 ml (½ pint) double cream

Hazelnut Praline:
50 g (2 oz) sugar
40 g (1½ oz) hazelnuts

Raspberry Sauce:
150 g (5 oz) raspberries
icing sugar, to taste

Mango Sauce:
1 mango, peeled, halved and stoned
squeeze of lemon juice

Put the single cream and sugar in a saucepan with the grated citrus rinds. Bring to the boil and sprinkle on the semolina, stirring well. Lower the heat and simmer for a few minutes, stirring. Soften the gelatine in a little cold water, then squeeze out excess water and add to the hot semolina, with the egg yolks, stirring well. Set aside to cool.

Whip the double cream until thick enough for the whisk to leave a ribbon trail on the surface when lifted. Fold into the cooled semolina.

Butter 4 ramekins or other individual moulds and fill with the semolina mixture. Chill in the refrigerator until firm.

For the hazelnut praline, put the sugar and hazelnuts in a heavy-based pan. Heat gently until the syrup melts, stirring frequently. Continue cooking over a medium-low heat until the syrup turns to a deep golden brown caramel. Immediately remove from the heat and pour onto an oiled marble slab or baking tray. Carefully spread out and leave to cool until set hard. Grind to a coarse powder in a food processor or blender.

For the raspberry sauce, purée the raspberries in a blender or food processor, then sieve to remove the pips. Sweeten with icing sugar to taste.

For the mango sauce, roughly chop the mango and purée until smooth.

To serve, invert the puddings onto individual serving plates and sprinkle with a little hazelnut praline. Surround with the raspberry and mango sauces.

THE HOME COUNTIES

DAVID HICKIN • KEELY SMITH • KEVIN SUMNER

PANEL OF JUDGES

Annie Wayte • Nicky Clarke • Loyd Grossman

WINNER

DAVID HICKIN'S MENU

STARTER

Cappuccino of Parsley with Pernod-seared Scallops

"The taste of the parsley was superb" **Annie Wayte**

MAIN COURSE

Fillet of Lamb with Apple and Celeriac Rösti, Caramelised Vegetables and a Madeira Sauce

"The whole dish I thought was superb... I couldn't really fault it" **Annie Wayte**

DESSERT

Tarte Citron with Lime Sauce

"The tarte citron was perfect. You could not improve it in any conceivable way" **Loyd**

David is a partner in a landscape gardening company which has contracts with many of Greater London's prestigious hotels. He takes full advantage of their leisure facilities for both business briefings and the odd game of snooker at which he is something of an expert! At home, David has an impressive collection of 78 rpm records and several period gramophones.

CAPPUCCINO OF PARSLEY WITH PERNOD-SEARED SCALLOPS

30 ml (2 tbsp) olive oil
1 small onion, finely chopped
1 clove garlic, finely chopped
1 potato, peeled and chopped
2 leeks, trimmed and chopped
salt and freshly ground black pepper
125 g (4 oz) parsley sprigs
600 ml (1 pint) chicken stock
150 ml (¼ pint) double cream
1.25 ml (¼ tsp) English mustard
4 scallops, cleaned
45 ml (3 tbsp) Pernod

Heat 15 ml (1 tbsp) oil in a medium saucepan, add the onion and garlic and fry gently for 5-10 minutes until softened. Meanwhile, cook the potato and leeks in boiling salted water to cover for 10 minutes or until softened; drain.

Put the potato and leek mixture in a blender or food processor with the parsley, and onion and garlic mixture. Process until fairly smooth, adding the stock through the feeder tube.

Blend in the cream and mustard, then season with salt and pepper to taste. Return to the clean saucepan.

Oil a griddle with the remaining 15 ml (1 tbsp) oil and sprinkle with the Pernod. Place over a high heat. Cut each scallop in half. When the griddle is very hot, add the scallops and sear quickly over a high heat for about 40 seconds, turning once.

Meanwhile, reheat the "cappuccino" and whisk to form a froth. Divide between warmed soup cups or bowls and add the scallops. Serve at once.

FILLET OF LAMB WITH APPLE AND CELERIAC RÖSTI

2 lamb (loin) fillets, each about 225 g (8 oz)
35-40 ml (1-2 tbsp, plus 2 tsp) olive oil
4 rosemary sprigs
120 ml (4 fl oz) Madeira
450 ml (¾ pint) lamb stock
50 g (2 oz) butter, in pieces
10 ml (2 tsp) chopped mint
2 black olives, stoned and chopped

Rösti:
2 potatoes
½ celeriac
1 apple, cored
salt and freshly ground black pepper
30 ml (2 tbsp) olive oil

Glazed Vegetables:
50 g (2 oz) butter
30 ml (2 tbsp) sugar
8 button onions
12 baby carrots
8 broccoli florets
8 cauliflower florets
8 sugar snap peas

Leek Garnish:
1 leek, trimmed
oil for deep-frying

First prepare the rösti. Peel and coarsely grate the potatoes, celeriac and apple. Mix together in a bowl and season with salt and pepper. Divide into 4 portions and shape into 7.5 cm (3 inch) rounds.

Cut the leek into long, thin shreds and set aside for the garnish.

To cook the rösti, heat 30 ml (2 tbsp) olive oil in a heavy-based frying pan. Place the rösti in the pan and cook for 10-15 minutes, pressing well down with a fish slice and turning halfway through cooking, until crisp and golden brown.

Meanwhile, heat 30 ml (2 tbsp) olive oil in another heavy-based frying pan with the rosemary sprigs. Add the lamb fillets and cook over a high heat, turning constantly, for 5-8 minutes until evenly browned, but still pink inside.

In the meantime, for the vegetables, add the butter and sugar to a medium saucepan containing a 2.5 cm (1 inch) depth of water and bring to the boil.

Transfer the cooked lamb to a warmed dish, cover and leave to rest in a warm place while preparing the sauce. Deglaze the meat pan with the Madeira, stirring to scrape up the sediment, then add the stock and boil steadily to reduce to the desired consistency.

Meanwhile, add the vegetables to the boiling water and cook for 3-4 minutes until just tender, then drain. Heat the oil for deep-frying and deep-fry the leek for 1 minute; drain on kitchen paper.

To finish the sauce, whisk in the butter a piece at a time. Mix the chopped mint and olives with 5-10 ml (1-2 tsp) olive oil and stir into the sauce.

To serve, place a rösti in the middle of each serving plate. Cut each lamb fillet into 4 thick slices and arrange on the rösti. Top with the leek and surround with the sauce and glazed vegetables.

TARTE CITRON WITH LIME SAUCE

The pastry used for these individual flans is quite fragile and should be handled as little as possible. You will need to mould it into the flan tins using your fingertips rather than roll it out.

Pastry:
160 g (5½ oz) butter
125 g (4 oz) icing sugar
1½ eggs (size 2), beaten
5 ml (1 tsp) lemon juice
300 g (10 oz) plain flour

Filling:
300 ml (½ pint) milk
1 vanilla pod, split
4 eggs (size 2)
50 g (2 oz) caster sugar
50 g (2 oz) plain flour
juice of 1 lemon
4 drops of vanilla essence

Sauce:
4 limes
1 lemon
50 g (2 oz) sugar
1 glass Sauternes wine
10 ml (2 tsp) arrowroot, mixed with a little water

To Serve:
selection of soft fruits (eg strawberries, raspberries and blueberries)
icing sugar, for dusting

To prepare the pastry, cream the butter and icing sugar together in a bowl until smooth. Add the eggs and beat thoroughly. Add the lemon juice, then the flour. Mix to a smooth paste. Wrap in cling film and chill in the refrigerator for 20 minutes.

Meanwhile, for the filling, warm the milk in a saucepan, add the vanilla pod and set aside to infuse for 15 minutes.

Divide the pastry into 4 portions. Press each portion into a round and use to line lightly greased 10 cm (4 inch) individual flan tins. Line with greaseproof paper and baking beans and bake blind in a preheated oven at 190°C (375°F) mark 5 for 15 minutes. Remove the paper and beans and bake for a further 5 minutes or until the base is cooked. Allow to cool, then remove the pastry cases from the tins.

To make the filling, bring the milk just to the boil, then remove the vanilla pod. Meanwhile, whisk the eggs and sugar together in a bowl until pale and thick, then whisk in the flour. Gradually whisk in the hot milk, then return the mixture to the pan. Bring to the boil, whisking all the time. Cook gently, whisking constantly, for about 2 minutes until the pastry cream is thickened (and no longer tastes floury). Remove from the heat and stir in the lemon juice and vanilla essence. Allow to cool.

Meanwhile, using a zester, pare thin strips of rind from one of the limes, blanch in boiling water for 1 minute, drain and set aside. To make the sauce, squeeze the juice from the limes and lemon and place in a saucepan with the sugar and 300 ml (½ pint) water. Heat gently until the sugar is dissolved, then add the wine, increase the heat and boil for 1 minute. Stir in the blended arrowroot and cook, stirring, until the sauce is slightly thickened and clear. Stir in the blanched lemon rind shreds and allow to cool.

Divide the pastry cream between the flan cases and place on individual serving plates. Surround with the lime sauce and arrange the fruit on top. Dust with icing sugar and serve immediately.

*Iced Passion Fruit Soufflé in a Caramel Cage,
with Glazed Strawberries*

GILL TUNKLE'S DESSERT (Regional Heat)

Scallop Mousseline inlaid with Crab,
served with Little Tartlets of Jerusalem Artichoke Purée

MARION MACFARLANE'S STARTER (Regional Heat)

*Salmon Fillet on a bed of Courgette and Ginger,
with an Orange Butter Sauce*

CLARE ASKAROFF'S MAIN COURSE (Regional Heat)

*Fillet of Lamb wrapped in Spinach and Prosciutto,
served with Potato and Herb Layers and Mediterranean Vegetables*

JOANNA CROSSLEY'S MAIN COURSE (Regional Heat)

THE HOME COUNTIES

DAVID HICKIN • KEELY SMITH • KEVIN SUMNER

PANEL OF JUDGES

Annie Wayte • Nicky Clarke • Loyd Grossman

KEELY SMITH'S MENU

STARTER

Garlic and Vermouth Mushrooms,
served with Cheese and Chive Soda Bread

MAIN COURSE

Guinea Fowl in Red Wine with Chestnuts

Braised Red Cabbage

Parmesan Parsnips

Dauphinoise Potatoes

"The dauphinoise were good" **Nicky Clarke**

DESSERT

Chocolate and Amaretto Cheese Tart

"That was great – the mixture of cheese, it just kept it from
being too sickly sweet" **Nicky Clarke**

"I liked the robustness of the whole menu" **Nicky Clarke**

Keely Smith lives in Bishop's Stortford and works at a major food
retailing distribution centre in Harlow. Keely is a keen
photographer, developing and printing her own portrait shots.
She's also a keep-fit fanatic and regularly works out at the
Harlow Pool Health Club.

Garlic and Vermouth Mushrooms

50 g (2 oz) butter
450 g (1 lb) mushrooms, trimmed
6 cloves garlic, crushed
salt and freshly ground black pepper
150 ml (¼ pint) Noilly Prat or dry vermouth
5 ml (1 tsp) cornflour
60 ml (4 tbsp) single cream
snipped chives, to garnish

Melt the butter in a large saucepan. Add the mushrooms with the garlic, salt and pepper, and Noilly Prat. Cover and simmer over a medium heat for 10-15 minutes, stirring occasionally.

Mix the cornflour with a little cold water to form a paste. Add to the mushroom mixture, stirring continuously. Cook, stirring, until slightly thickened. Leave to cool slightly, then stir in the cream. Serve garnished with snipped chives and accompanied by the Cheese and Chive Soda Bread.

Cheese and Chive Soda Bread

350 g (12 oz) plain flour
2.5 ml (½ tsp) bicarbonate of soda
2.5 ml (½ tsp) salt
1.25 ml (¼ tsp) baking powder
15 g (½ oz) butter
25 g (1 oz) mature Cheddar cheese, grated
30 ml (2 tbsp) snipped chives
150-300 ml (¼-½ pint) milk

Mix all the dry ingredients together in a bowl. Rub in the butter, then add the cheese and chives. Stir in enough milk to make a medium-soft dough.

Knead the dough lightly and split into 4 equal portions. Shape into rolls and place on a lightly oiled baking sheet. Bake in a preheated oven at 220°C (425°F) mark 7 for 25-30 minutes. Serve warm, with the mushrooms.

GUINEA FOWL IN RED WINE WITH CHESTNUTS

Get your poulterer or butcher to bone the guinea fowl for you, remembering to ask for the carcasses which you will need for the stock.

4 guinea fowl breasts

Stock:
30 ml (2 tbsp) olive oil
2 guinea fowl carcasses
2 onions, roughly chopped
2 carrots, roughly chopped
½ bottle full-bodied red wine
5 ml (1 tsp) juniper berries
1 bay leaf
bouquet garni

To Finish:
15 ml (1 tbsp) olive oil
¼ bottle full-bodied red wine
300 ml (½ pint) guinea fowl stock
30 ml (2 tbsp) black treacle
1 bay leaf
225 g (8 oz) frozen chestnuts, defrosted
salt and freshly ground black pepper
10 ml (2 tsp) arrowroot

First make the stock. Heat the oil in a large pan, add the guinea fowl carcasses and brown well. Add the onions and carrots and sauté until lightly browned. Add 600 ml (1 pint) water and all the other stock ingredients. Bring to the boil, lower the heat and simmer gently for about 3 hours.

Strain the stock into a bowl and allow to cool. Refrigerate when cold so that the fat sets on the surface. Discard this fat layer before use.

To cook the guinea fowl, heat the oil in a heavy-based frying pan over a medium-high heat. Add the guinea fowl breasts and brown on both sides. Add the wine, stock, treacle, bay leaf, chest-nuts and salt and pepper. Bring to the boil, lower the heat and simmer for 15-20 minutes.

Mix the arrowroot to a paste with a little cold water. Remove the guinea fowl breasts from the pan and keep warm. Add the arrowroot paste to the sauce, stirring continuously. Cook, stirring, for 2-3 minutes.

To serve, slice the guinea fowl breasts and arrange on warmed individual serving plates with the chestnuts. Spoon over the sauce and serve at once, with the accompaniments.

BRAISED RED CABBAGE

15 ml (1 tbsp) oil
1 small onion, thinly sliced
1 small red cabbage, finely shredded
1 cooking apple, peeled, cored and chopped
30 ml (2 tbsp) balsamic vinegar
45 ml (3 tbsp) soft brown sugar
salt and freshly ground black pepper

Heat the oil in a saucepan, add the onion and fry over a gentle heat for about 5 minutes. Add the cabbage, apple, vinegar and 60 ml (4 tbsp) water to the pan. Stir well and cook gently until the mixture begins to soften. Add the sugar and seasoning; mix well.

Cover and simmer for 30 minutes, stirring from time to time. Add 30-45 ml (2-3 tbsp) water if the mixture shows signs of becoming dry. Cook for a further 30 minutes or until the cabbage is tender. Taste and adjust the seasoning. Serve immediately.

PARMESAN PARSNIPS

450 g (1 lb) parsnips, peeled and quartered
salt
60 ml (4 tbsp) olive oil
freshly grated nutmeg
125 g (4 oz) Parmesan cheese, freshly grated

Heat the oil in a roasting tin in a preheated oven at 180°C (350°F) mark 4. Meanwhile, parboil the parsnips in salted water for about 5 minutes. Drain and transfer to the roasting tin. Sprinkle with nutmeg and bake for 20 minutes.

Sprinkle with the Parmesan and bake for a further 20 minutes or until crisp and brown. Serve immediately.

DAUPHINOISE POTATOES

25 g (1 oz) butter
1 small onion, thinly sliced
1 clove garlic, crushed
450 g (1 lb) King Edward potatoes, peeled
  and thinly sliced
150 ml (¼ pint) double cream
a little milk
salt and freshly ground black pepper

Melt half of the butter in a saucepan, add the onion and garlic and cook until soft.

Grease a suitable dish with the remaining butter. Layer a third of the potatoes in the base of the dish. Cover with half of the onion and garlic, then pour on half of the cream and milk; season liberally. Repeat these layers and finish with a layer of potatoes.

Cover with foil and bake in a preheated oven at 180°C (350°F) mark 4 for 45 minutes. Remove the foil and bake for a further 15 minutes until brown. Serve immediately.

CHOCOLATE AND AMARETTO CHEESE TART

225 g (8 oz) chocolate digestive biscuits
50 g (2 oz) butter, melted
2 eggs
225 g (8 oz) cream cheese
25 g (1 oz) caster sugar
150 ml (¼ pint) double cream
125 g (4 oz) good quality plain chocolate
60 ml (4 tbsp) amaretto di Saronno liqueur
toasted flaked almonds, to decorate

Grease 4 small clean baked bean tins, or similar ovenproof moulds. Finely crush the biscuits and mix with the melted butter. Spoon into the greased tins and press down firmly onto the bases, using the back of the spoon. Chill in the refrigerator while preparing the topping.

Place the eggs, cream cheese, sugar and cream in a food processor and process for 15 seconds.

Meanwhile, break the chocolate into pieces, place in a pyrex bowl and melt in the microwave on MEDIUM for 3 minutes. (Alternatively stand the bowl over a pan of simmering water until melted.) Let cool slightly, then add to the cream mixture, with the liqueur. Process for a further 10 seconds until evenly mixed.

Pour the mixture on top of the biscuit bases and bake in a preheated oven at 150°C (300°F) mark 2 for 15-25 minutes until just set. Remove from the oven and chill in the refrigerator for at least 1 hour.

Run a knife around the edge of each tart and carefully remove from their tins. Decorate with the toasted almonds and serve with single cream.

Note: When cooked, the tarts may have an uneven surface. Trim to level if necessary after turning out.

THE HOME COUNTIES

DAVID HICKIN • KEELY SMITH • KEVIN SUMNER

PANEL OF JUDGES

Annie Wayte • Nicky Clarke • Loyd Grossman

KEVIN SUMNER'S MENU

STARTER

King Prawn and Papaya Salad

"The quality of the papaya and the prawns were really nice" **Annie Wayte**

MAIN COURSE

Stuffed Saddle of Rabbit

Potato Rösti and Spinach

Sautéed Mushrooms

"The rabbit I thought was divine, and particularly the chanterelles were really exquisite" **Nicky Clarke**

DESSERT

Cold Lemon Soufflé
in a Brandy Snap Basket with a Lemon and Lime Sauce

"The flavours were there, excellent" **Annie Wayte**

Kevin Sumner from Watford is an actor by profession. He features in several long-running series as well as the odd commercial. Kevin's big passion is motor racing, and he is the mechanic for a successful Mini 7 race team regularly performing at Brand's Hatch and Silverstone. Kevin also enjoys badminton and partnered by his wife, Helen, plays competitively at the Watford Leisure Centre.

KING PRAWN AND PAPAYA SALAD

12 raw king prawns, shelled, de-veined and
 rinsed
45 ml (3 tbsp) olive oil
225 g (8 oz) raspberries
1 papaya
125 g (4 oz) smoked back bacon, derinded

To Serve:
300 g (10 oz) mixed salad leaves (eg rocket,
 watercress and frisée)

Put the prawns in a bowl, pour on the olive oil and set aside until ready to cook.

Purée the raspberries in a food processor, then pass through a fine sieve to remove the pips.

Cut the papaya into quarters, scoop out the seeds and remove the skin. Slice each quarter lengthwise, leaving the tip intact to form a fan.

Remove the fat from the bacon, then grill until crispy. Chop into small pieces.

Cook the prawns under a preheated grill, for about 2-3 minutes, turning occasionally, until pink.

To serve, arrange a portion of salad leaves in the middle of each serving plate. Place a papaya fan to one side. Sprinkle some of the crispy bacon over the salad and top with the prawns. Pour on a little of the raspberry purée and serve immediately.

STUFFED SADDLE OF RABBIT

2 saddles of rabbit (with liver and kidneys)
25 ml (1 fl oz) groundnut oil
salt and freshly ground black pepper
1 tarragon sprig
1 rosemary sprig
4 pieces of pigs' caul, soaked in cold water

Rabbit Gravy:
450 ml (¾ pint) rabbit stock
10 ml (2 tsp) rowan jelly
15 g (½ oz) unsalted butter

Remove the kidneys from the saddles and carefully peel off the outer membrane. Heat the oil in a frying pan. Add the rabbit kidneys and liver and cook gently for 2 minutes, turning once. Remove from the pan. Halve the kidneys and cut the liver into small pieces.

Remove the bone from the saddles of rabbit and open the meat out flat on a board. Lightly season with salt and pepper. Roughly chop the herbs and sprinkle over the saddles. Place some chopped liver and 2 kidney slices on each saddle. Roll up each saddle piece, being careful not to squeeze out the filling. Wrap each one in a piece of pigs' caul.

Place the saddles in a small roasting tin and stand in a larger tin. Pour boiling water into the outer tin to come halfway up the sides. Roast in a preheated oven at 220°C (425°F) mark 7 for 12-15 minutes.

Meanwhile make the gravy. Gently heat the stock in a small saucepan until simmering, then add the rowan jelly. When the jelly has melted into the stock, whisk in the butter. Season with salt and pepper to taste.

Remove the rabbit from the oven and leave to rest in a warm place for a few minutes. To serve, slice the saddles of rabbit and arrange on individual serving plates. Pour the gravy over the rabbit and serve at once, with the accompaniments.

POTATO RÖSTI AND SPINACH

225 g (8 oz) potatoes
1 clove garlic, crushed
freshly grated nutmeg
salt and freshly ground black pepper
15 ml (1 tbsp) groundnut oil
25 g (1 oz) unsalted butter
225 g (8 oz) spinach, trimmed

Peel and grate the potatoes and rinse in cold water. Drain and pat dry with kitchen paper. Put the potatoes in a bowl with the crushed garlic, nutmeg and seasoning.

Heat a large frying pan and add the oil and half of the butter. Position 4 non-stick 7.5 cm (3 inch) metal rings in the frying pan. Fill with the potato mixture and press down. Fry for about 3 minutes, then remove the rings and turn the potato rösti over; fry for a further 3 minutes. Drain on kitchen paper.

Steam the spinach in a covered saucepan with just the water clinging to the leaves after washing for 2 minutes. Drain the spinach and squeeze out all the liquid. Chop the spinach and mix with the remaining butter, some nutmeg and seasoning.

Put the 4 metal rings on a baking sheet lined with non-stick baking parchment and fill with the spinach. Cook in a preheated oven at 200°C (400°F) mark 6 for 5-10 minutes, until heated through. Remove the rings and transfer to warmed serving plates. Top with the rösti.

SAUTÉED MUSHROOMS

125 g (4 oz) chanterelles
15 ml (1 tbsp) unsalted butter
15 ml (1 tbsp) dry sherry
salt and freshly ground black pepper

Put the chanterelles in a small saucepan and dry-fry for 2 minutes, shaking the pan frequently. Add the butter and sauté for a further 3 minutes. Add the sherry and season with salt and pepper. Serve immediately.

COLD LEMON SOUFFLÉ WITH A LEMON AND LIME SAUCE

Lemon Soufflé:
15 g (½ oz) sachet gelatine
finely grated rind and juice of 1½ lemons
2 eggs, separated
125 g (4 oz) caster sugar
150 ml (¼ pint) double cream

Lemon and Lime Sauce:
125 g (4 oz) caster sugar
finely pared zest and juice of 1 lemon
finely pared zest and juice of 1 lime
5 ml (1 tsp) arrowroot

To Serve:
Brandy Snap Baskets (see right)

For the soufflé, sprinkle the gelatine over 30 ml (2 tbsp) cold water in a cup. Put the lemon rind and juice in a large bowl with the egg yolks and sugar. Stand the bowl over a saucepan of simmering water and whisk until the mixture turns pale and starts to thicken. Remove the bowl from the pan.

Stand the cup of gelatine in the saucepan of hot water until it has dissolved, then add to the egg yolk mixture, stirring well.

In a separate bowl, whip the cream until soft peaks form. In another bowl, whisk the egg whites until stiff. Allow the egg yolk mixture to cool, stirring occasionally, then fold in the cream, followed by the egg whites. Pour into individual moulds and chill in the refrigerator for at least 1½ hours.

Meanwhile, make the lemon and lime sauce. Put the sugar and 120 ml (4 fl oz) water in a small pan and heat gently, stirring to help dissolve the sugar. Add the lemon and lime zests and simmer gently for 15 minutes. Mix the arrowroot with the lemon juice and half of the lime juice. Add to the pan and stir until it returns to

a simmer. Remove from the heat and leave to cool. Just before serving, stir in the rest of the lime juice.

To serve, position a brandy snap basket in the middle of each serving plate. Dip the soufflé moulds in a bowl of hot water for a few seconds, then turn out into the brandy snap baskets. Pour the lemon and lime sauce around the baskets. Serve at once.

BRANDY SNAP BASKETS

50 g (2 oz) butter
50 g (2 oz) caster sugar
30 ml (2 tbsp) golden syrup
5 ml (1 tsp) brandy
5 ml (1 tsp) lemon juice
60 ml (4 tbsp) plain flour
5 ml (1 tsp) ground ginger

Melt the butter in a saucepan, add the sugar and syrup, and heat gently until dissolved. Remove from the heat and add all the other ingredients. Mix well. For each basket, spread 30 ml (2 tbsp) of the mixture into a round, about 12 cm (5 inches) in diameter on a baking sheet lined with non-stick baking parchment. (Shape and bake 2 baskets at a time.)

Cook in a preheated oven at 180°C (350°F) mark 4 for 6-8 minutes. Leave for 20 seconds, then remove the brandy snap using a palette knife and lay over an upturned ramekin. Shape to form a basket, then allow to cool.

DEREK MORRIS • MARK ARGENT • JENNI GUY

PANEL OF JUDGES

Terry Laybourne • Rosemary Leach • Loyd Grossman

WINNER

DEREK MORRIS' MENU

STARTER

*Brochettes of Monkfish
with Florence Fennel and Star Anise*

MAIN COURSE

Smoked Chicken Boudin

Caramelised Apple

Potato and Watercress Purée

Julienne of Celeriac with Dijon Mustard

DESSERT

Walnut Pie with a Prune and Marsala Sauce

"The pudding was not too rich, and the pastry was just divine" **Rosemary Leach**

"I thought as a menu it was very nice, very well balanced" **Terry Laybourne**

Derek Morris lives in the village of Lower Tasburgh in Norfolk. He is a professional sculptor and for 21 years was head of the faculty at Norwich School of Art. Derek is now involved with the King of Hearts, a privately run Norwich arts centre, where he curates many of the exhibitions of painting and sculpture. His wife, Christine, has a gift shop which specialises in doll's houses and furniture, and Derek helps out with the stocktaking and accounts.

BROCHETTES OF MONKFISH WITH FLORENCE FENNEL AND STAR ANISE

350 g (12 oz) monkfish fillet
30 ml (2 tbsp) Greek yogurt
2.5 ml (½ tsp) ground star anise
350 g (12 oz) Florence fennel
15 ml (1 tbsp) sunflower oil
sea salt
freshly ground black pepper

To Serve:
1 small red pepper, halved, cored, deseeded
* and thinly sliced*
a little oil
roasted sesame seeds, for sprinkling
fennel or parsley leaves, to garnish

Remove the skin from the fish, then cut into 2 cm (¾ inch) cubes and place in a bowl. Add the yogurt and star anise powder and stir to coat each piece of fish with the mixture. Cover and leave to marinate for 1 hour.

Meanwhile trim the fennel bulbs, quarter, then cut crosswise into thin slices about 5 mm (¼ inch) thick. Heat the oil in a sauté pan. Add the fennel with about 30 ml (2 tbsp) water and a sprinkling of sea salt. Cover and cook over a medium heat for 5 minutes, then remove the lid, increase the heat and sauté until the fennel is browned. Remove from the pan and keep warm.

Thread the pieces of monkfish onto 8 wooden skewers, reserving the marinade. Cook under a preheated high grill for about 2 minutes each side until browned. Meanwhile, add the remaining marinade to the fennel with 15 ml (1 tbsp) water and heat through gently. Season with pepper.

Sauté the red pepper slices in a little oil until soft. To serve, divide the fennel between warmed serving plates and sprinkle with roasted sesame seeds. Place two brochettes on top of each mound of fennel and garnish with the red pepper slices and fennel or parsley leaves.

Note: To prevent scorching, pre-soak the kebab skewers in water.

SMOKED CHICKEN BOUDIN WITH CARAMELISED APPLE

For this recipe, you need a sausage-maker.

natural sausage skins
125 g (4 oz) smoked chicken breast
125 g (4 oz) pork loin
225 g (8 oz) hard pork fat
175 g (6 oz) onion, chopped
25 g (1 oz) white breadcrumbs
37 ml (2½ tbsp) single cream
1 egg, plus 1 egg yolk
7.5 ml (1½ tsp) sea salt
2.5 ml (½ tsp) ground white pepper
3.75 ml (¾ tsp) ground mixed spices (white
* pepper, cloves, nutmeg and cinnamon)*

Caramelised Apple:
1 large Cox's apple
15 g (½ oz) butter
10 ml (2 tsp) brown sugar

To Garnish:
radicchio leaves

First soak the sausage skins in cold water to cover. Chop the chicken, pork and pork fat into small cubes.

Blanch the onion in boiling water for 1 minute; drain thoroughly and let cool. Soak the breadcrumbs in the cream.

Place all the meat in a food processor, with the onion, soaked breadcrumbs, egg yolk, salt, pepper and spices. Process until smooth. Assemble the sausage-maker and slip the skins into place. Tie the end with cotton string and fill the skins; do not over-fill. Tie the other end and divide into 4 sausages with string.

Bring a large pan of water to simmering point and gently lower the boudin into it. Keep the water at a gentle simmer; it should be only just moving. Prick the sausages all over with a large needle as they rise to the surface. Cook for 20 minutes, then drain and separate.

Meanwhile, prepare the caramelised apple. Peel, quarter, core and slice the apple. Melt the butter in a non-stick frying pan and slice the apple into it. Sprinkle with the sugar and cook over a high heat until brown.

Place the boudin under a preheated hot grill and cook, turning, until browned all over. Serve the boudin on a bed of radicchio leaves. Garnish with the caramelised apple and serve with the accompaniments.

POTATO AND WATERCRESS PURÉE

675 g (1½ lb) Desirée or Romano Potatoes
sea salt
25 g (1 oz) butter
2 cloves garlic, finely chopped
75 ml (5 tbsp) milk
freshly ground black pepper
50 g (2 oz) watercress, trimmed and coarsely
  chopped

Peel and quarter the potatoes. Place in a saucepan and cover with cold water. Add salt. Bring to the boil and cook for about 20 minutes until tender. Drain and return to the saucepan.

Meanwhile, melt the butter in a small pan, add the garlic and cook over a low heat for 1 minute. Add the milk, bring to the boil, then pour onto the potatoes. Mash thoroughly, then beat with a wooden spoon. Check the seasoning. Stir in the watercress and serve the purée piping hot.

JULIENNE OF CELERIAC WITH DIJON MUSTARD

350 g (12 oz) celeriac
juice of ½ lemon
salt
30 ml (2 tbsp) double cream
15 ml (1 tbsp) wholegrain Dijon mustard

Peel the celeriac, cut into 3 mm (⅛ inch) thick slices, then into matchstick strips. Immediately immerse in a bowl of cold water acidulated with the lemon juice to prevent discolouration. Drain, then add to a pan of boiling salted water and cook for 2 minutes. Drain thoroughly. Mix the cream and mustard together, add to the celeriac and toss well. Serve at once.

WALNUT PIE WITH A PRUNE AND MARSALA SAUCE

Pastry:
250 g (9 oz) unbleached plain flour
25 g (1 oz) icing sugar
2.5 ml (½ tsp) salt
175 g (6 oz) cold unsalted butter, diced
1 (size 2) egg, plus 1 egg yolk

Filling:
150 g (5 oz) walnuts
2 (size 2) eggs
210 g (7½ oz) vanilla-flavoured caster sugar
1 egg yolk, mixed with a little milk

Prune and Marsala Sauce:
75 g (3 oz) Agen prunes, soaked overnight
in 300 ml (½ pint) water
45 ml (3 tbsp) Marsala
15 ml (1 tbsp) double cream
a little sugar, to taste

To Decorate:
icing sugar, for dusting
12 walnut halves

Sift the flour, icing sugar and salt into a mixing bowl. Add the butter and rub in until the mixture resembles breadcrumbs. Lightly beat the eggs and add to the flour mixture. Mix to a smooth dough, using a round-bladed knife. Wrap in cling film and leave to rest in the refrigerator for at least 30 minutes.

To make the filling, put the walnuts in a food processor or blender and grind to a medium fineness. Put the eggs and sugar in a mixing bowl and stir with a balloon whisk for 2 minutes, without beating. Stir in the ground walnuts.

Set aside one third of the pastry for the lid. Roll out the larger piece on a lightly floured surface until big enough to line an oblong loose-bottomed tart tin, measuring 36 x 11 cm (14 x 4½ inches). Line the tin with the pastry and trim the edges. (Add the trimmings to the other portion of pastry.) Fill with the walnut mixture.

Roll out the pastry to make a lid. Moisten the edges with a little of the egg mixture and carefully position the lid, pressing the edges together to seal. Trim off excess pastry. Make three slits in the lid and brush with the egg and milk. Bake in a preheated oven at 180°C (350°F) mark 4 for 35 minutes.

Meanwhile, make the sauce. Cook the prunes in the soaking water for 20 minutes or until soft. Allow to cool a little, then drain, reserving the liquor, and remove the stones. Press the flesh through a fine sieve with a wooden spoon. Put the prune pulp and Marsala in a blender and process until smooth adding enough prune juice to make a sauce the consistency of thin cream. Pour into a small bowl and stir in the cream. Adjust the sweetness if necessary, keeping the sauce slightly tart.

Allow the tart to cool, then remove from the tin. Dust with icing sugar and cut into thick slices. To serve, pour a pool of sauce onto each serving plate. Place a slice of walnut pie in the centre and decorate with walnut halves.

THE EAST

DEREK MORRIS • MARK ARGENT • JENNI GUY

PANEL OF JUDGES

Terry Laybourne • Rosemary Leach • Loyd Grossman

MARK ARGENT'S MENU

STARTER

Lobak

"It was different... there were flavours that I hadn't anticipated and I haven't encountered before. I did enjoy the Lobak" **Terry Laybourne**

MAIN COURSE

Spicy Chicken with Prawn Sambal

Sour-fried Vegetables

Nasi Lemak (Coconut Rice)

Ikan Bilis Goreng (Fried Dried Anchovies) and Peanuts

"It looked lovely" **Rosemary Leach**

DESSERT

Special Agar-agar with Fruit

"I enjoyed the dessert" **Terry Laybourne**

Mark Argent comes from Cambridge and is a music typesetter by profession. Chamber music is Mark's great love and he regularly plays the cello in a trio with friends at a converted chapel. He has recently written a biography about the organist RJS Stevens and the success of the book is encouraging him to seek out the manuscripts to research a sequel.

LOBAK

These quick-fried envelopes of crispy bean curd skin enclose a spicy minced pork filling. They are a popular South-East Asian snack/starter.

Filling:
80 g (3 oz) leek, trimmed and chopped
5 ml (1 tsp) peanut oil
5 ml (1 tsp) sesame oil
120 g (4 oz) cooked minced pork
5 water chestnuts, finely chopped
10 ml (2 tsp) five-spice powder
5 ml (1 tsp) katsup manis
5 ml (1 tsp) dark soy sauce
20 ml (4 tsp) dried shrimp
½ chilli, finely chopped
5 ml (1 tsp) sugar
1 egg, beaten

To Assemble:
4 pieces dried bean curd skin
5 ml (1 tsp) cornflour, mixed to a paste with a little water
vegetable oil for deep-frying

To Serve:
fish sauce
sliced chilli, to taste
sugar, to taste

Fry the leek in the peanut and sesame oils until tender. Mix together all of the ingredients for the filling in a bowl until evenly combined.

Dampen each piece of bean curd skin and place a strip of filling along one edge. Brush the other edges with the cornflour paste and roll up to enclose the filling and form a sausage shape.

Heat the oil for deep-frying and deep-fry the rolls until crisp and golden brown. Drain on kitchen paper.

Serve cool, cut into slices and accompanied by the fish sauce, flavoured with chilli and sugar to taste.

SPICY CHICKEN

For this dish, you will need to prepare a rich stock in advance.

2 chickens, each about 1.1 kg (2½ lb)

Stock Flavourings:
3 cloves garlic
1 star anise
4 cloves
5 cm (2 inch) cinnamon stick
1 stalk lemon grass
5 chillis
2 cm (¾ inch) fresh root ginger
2 small onions, peeled
40 g (1½ oz) coriander seeds
5 ml (1 tsp) cumin seeds
10 ml (2 tsp) fish sauce

Spice Paste:
10 ml (2 tsp) cumin seeds
10 ml (2 tsp) szechuan peppercorns
10 ml (2 tsp) coriander seeds
10 ml (2 tsp) powdered cinnamon
1 stalk lemon grass
3 chillis
1 clove garlic, peeled

To Finish:
3 potatoes, peeled
50 g (2 oz) santan powder (dried coconut milk), approximately
2 tomatoes, chopped
a little cornflour, for coating
10 ml (2 tsp) fish sauce (approximately)
powdered cinnamon, to taste

To prepare the stock, joint the chicken and set aside about 550 g (1¼ lb) of the meat from the thighs, breast and/or leg. Put the chicken carcasses and remaining meat into a saucepan with the stock flavouring ingredients. Add sufficient water to cover and bring to the boil. Lower the heat, cover and simmer for at least 3 hours. Strain the stock, discarding the chicken and spices, allow to cool, then refrigerate.

Meanwhile, cut the reserved chicken meat into bite-sized pieces and toss in a shallow dish with 22 ml (1½ tbsp) of the fish sauce. Set aside to marinate.

To prepare the spice paste, roast the cumin seeds, szechuan peppercorns and coriander seeds, then pound together with the other spices, using a pestle and mortar or a spice grinder. Add half of this paste to the marinating chicken.

About 1 hour before serving, skim off the fat from the chicken stock and use a little of it to fry the remaining spice paste in a heavy-based pan for 1-2 minutes. Add the stock and bring to a simmer. Finely chop one of the potatoes; cut the rest into large chunks; add both to the pan.

After a while, add the santan to taste, together with the tomatoes.

About 10-15 minutes before serving, rub a little cornflour into the marinating meat and add to the stock, with the marinade. Adjust the flavour with fish sauce and cinnamon to taste. Serve with the accompaniments.

PRAWN SAMBAL

1 chilli
7 shallots
7.5 ml (1½ tsp) turmeric powder
2.5 cm (1 inch) fresh root ginger
15 ml (1 tbsp) peanut oil
1 onion, finely chopped
150 g (5 oz) tiger prawns, shelled and
   deveined
5 ml (1 tsp) Malaysian prawn paste
   (approximately)
50 g (2 oz) tomato purée (approximately)
5 ml (1 tsp) sugar
5 ml (1 tsp) cornflour, mixed with a little
   water (optional)

Pound the chilli, shallots, turmeric and ginger together, using a pestle and mortar or spice grinder. Heat the peanut oil in a heavy-based frying pan. Add the spice mixture and fry, stirring, for about 1 minute. Add the onion and fry gently until softened. Add the prawns and continue to fry until they are cooked through.

Mix the prawn paste with a little boiling water, then add to the pan with the tomato puree and sugar, adjusting the quantities according to taste. If necessary, thicken the sambal with a little cornflour paste. Reheat before serving.

NASI LEMAK

350 g (12 oz) Thai fragrant rice
salt
65 (2½ oz) santen powder
1 pandan leaf

Put the rice in a rice cooker and add sufficient cold water to cover the rice by 1 cm (½ inch). Add the salt, santen and panden leaf. Bring to the boil, stirring once or twice, lower the heat and simmer until all the water is absorbed and the rice is tender. Stir a few times during cooking and add a little extra water if necessary. Discard the pandan leaf before serving.

IKAN BILIS GORENG

45 ml (3 tbsp) dried ikan bilis (small dried
   salted fish)
peanut oil, for frying

Rinse the ikan bilis in cold water and dry on kitchen paper. Heat a little peanut oil in a wok or heavy-based frying pan, add the ikan bilis and fry, stirring, over a moderate heat until crispy. Drain on kitchen paper.

SOUR-FRIED VEGETABLES

1 clove garlic, chopped
peanut oil, for frying
3 carrots, peeled and cut into strips
120 g (4 oz) mangetouts
½-1 sour mango, peeled, stoned and chopped
1 slice terasi (balachan - a pungent shrimp paste), roasted and pounded
katsup manis, to taste
dark soy sauce, to taste
lime juice, to taste (optional)

Using the same wok or pan used for the ikan bilis, fry the garlic in a little peanut oil for about 1 minute, then add the carrots and fry until slightly softened. Add the mangetout and fry for about 1 minute, then add the sour mango, terasi, katsup manis, soy sauce and lime juice to taste (see note). Cook until the vegetables and mango are tender. Serve hot.

Note: Sour mangos vary in size and flavour. If not sufficiently sour, you will need to adjust the flavour with lime juice.

SPECIAL AGAR-AGAR WITH FRUIT

40 g (1½ oz) rock sugar
14 cm (6 inch) agar-agar strip
1 pandan leaf
juice of 1 lime
4 drops of pandan essence
juice of ½ lemon
3 pinches of salt
granulated or rock sugar, to taste
16 longans
24 raspberries
2 sharp kiwi fruit

Chill 4 serving glasses in the refrigerator. Meanwhile, put the rock sugar, agar-agar strip, pandan leaf and the juice of ½ lime in a saucepan with 360 ml (12 fl oz) water. Bring to a simmer and simmer gently until the agar dissolves.

Put 1 drop of pandan essence in the base of each serving glass and add 5 ml (1 tsp) of the hot agar-agar solution. Stir, then allow to cool and set.

Add a further 360 ml (12 fl oz) water to the agar-agar solution, together with the rest of the lime juice, the lemon juice, the salt and sugar to taste. Take out a little of the solution and test for setting on a cold spoon: it should be softly set with a clean, refreshing taste. Strain the agar-agar solution; keep hot.

Halve 12 longans. Pour a 1.5 cm (¾ inch) depth of agar-agar solution and drop 6 longan halves into each serving glass. Allow to set.

When just set, pour on a thin layer of agar-agar solution. Arrange 6 raspberries around the edge of each glass and intersperse with halved kiwi slices. Place a longan in the centre.

Glaze with a little more agar-agar solution. Chill before serving.

THE EAST

DEREK MORRIS • MARK ARGENT • JENNI GUY

PANEL OF JUDGES

Terry Laybourne • Rosemary Leach • Loyd Grossman

JENNI GUY'S MENU

STARTER

*Warm Salad of Griddled Scallops
with a Saffron Dressing*

"I did like the starter. It looks very pleasant…
and not too heavy" **Rosemary Leach**

MAIN COURSE

*Medallions of Lamb
with a Port and Redcurrant Sauce*

Potatoes Dauphinoise

Seasonal Vegetables

"The potatoes were exceptional. The lamb works well with
a sweet sauce" **Terry Laybourne**

DESSERT

*Dark Chocolate Cheesecake,
served with a Bitter Orange Sauce and Citrus Cream*

"The chocolate cheesecake is wonderful" **Rosemary Leach**

Jenni Guy comes from Ipswich and works with a charity called
Suffolk Carers Support, which provides help for those who care
for disabled relatives. She's an enthusiastic collector of antiques, and
spends many a happy day bargain hunting at the local auctions. Jenni's
daughter, Jessie, has just starting riding, which gives Jenni the opportunity for some long country walks.

WARM SALAD OF GRIDDLED SCALLOPS WITH A SAFFRON DRESSING

16 small scallops, cleaned
2 heads of chicory
1 head of radicchio
2 red peppers
2 yellow peppers
2 large courgettes
1 large carrot (optional)
knob of butter
4 rashers smoked streaky bacon, derinded
  and diced
60 ml (4 tbsp) olive oil
2 cloves garlic, crushed

Dressing:

2 pinches of saffron strands
150 ml (¼ pint) white wine
375 ml (13 fl oz) fish stock
juice of 1 lemon
pinch of cayenne pepper
120 ml (4 fl oz) apple juice
2 shallots, chopped

To Garnish:

salad leaves

To make the dressing, put all of the ingredients in a saucepan and bring to the boil. Cook over a moderate heat for 15-20 minutes until the liquid has reduced by about half.

Meanwhile, slice the scallops into rounds. Chop the chicory and radicchio into bite-sized pieces. Halve, core and deseed the peppers, then cut into thin strips.

Using a swivel vegetable peeler, pare the courgette lengthwise into long ribbons. Do the same with the carrot, if using.

Heat a knob of butter in a frying pan, add the bacon and fry until cooked and crisp; keep warm.

Heat the oil in a large frying pan, add the garlic and all of the vegetables and fry, stirring, for 3-4 minutes, until just tender.

Preheat a griddle, or the grill to high. Add the scallops and cook using a high heat, for 2-3 minutes, or until slightly tinged brown.

Pile the vegetables onto warmed serving plates, lay the scallops on top and sprinkle with the crispy bacon pieces. Pour on the hot dressing and garnish with salad leaves. Serve immediately.

Note: Served with fresh crusty bread or ciabatta, this makes a good, light lunch.

MEDALLIONS OF LAMB WITH PORT AND REDCURRANT SAUCE

Ask your butcher to bone the lamb for you. Use the bones to make a well-flavoured stock for the sauce.

1.2 kg (2½ lb) best end of lamb, boned
salt and freshly ground black pepper
30 ml (2 tbsp) olive oil

Sauce:
300 ml (½ pint) homemade lamb stock
150 ml (¼ pint) ruby port
125 g (4 oz) redcurrant jelly
juice of 1 orange
5 ml (1 tsp) arrowroot (optional)

To Garnish:
redcurrants (optional)

Trim the lamb if necessary and season with salt and pepper.

To make the sauce, pour the lamb stock into a saucepan and bring to the boil. Boil steadily until reduced by about half. Add the port and boil to reduce further. Whisk in the redcurrant jelly until amalgamated, then add the orange juice. The sauce should be thick enough to lightly coat the back of a spoon. If it requires thickening, mix the arrowroot with a little water, stir into the sauce and cook, stirring, for 1-2 minutes until thickened and translucent. Set aside.

Heat the oil in a heavy-based pan until hot, then add the lamb and quickly seal until browned on all sides. Transfer the meat to an ovenproof tin and cook in a preheated oven at 230°C (450°F) mark 8 for 15-20 minutes. Wrap in foil and leave to rest in a warm place for 5-10 minutes.

To serve, carve the lamb into slices and arrange on warmed serving plates. Garnish with redcurrants if desired.

POTATOES DAUPHINOISE

625 g (1 lb 6 oz) medium potatoes
salt and freshly ground black pepper
½ clove garlic
600 ml (1 pint) double cream
60 ml (4 tbsp) milk

Peel the potatoes, rinse and slice thinly. Spread out on a tea-towel and sprinkle with salt; leave for 10 minutes. Rub a gratin dish with the clove of garlic.

Mix the cream and milk together with a little salt and pepper. Bring to the boil and boil for 2 minutes.

Pat the potatoes dry with kitchen paper, then add to the boiling milk mixture. Transfer to the prepared dish and spread evenly. Bake in a preheated oven at 170°C (325°F) mark 3 for 45 minutes or until crisp and brown on top, and the potato layers underneath are tender.

DARK CHOCOLATE CHEESECAKE

This cheesecake is delicious served still slightly warm, but it can be kept in the refrigerator for up to 2 days. If preferred make individual cheesecakes (see note).

Praline:
125 g (4 oz) pistachio nuts
125 g (4 oz) sugar

Base:
150 g (5 oz) digestive biscuits, finely crushed
100 g (3½ oz) butter, melted
125 g (4 oz) pistachio praline (see above)

Filling:
2 eggs, separated
75 g (3 oz) caster sugar
225 g (8 oz) full-fat soft cheese
25 g (1 oz) ground almonds
150 ml (¼ pint) milk
25 g (1 oz) cocoa powder, sifted

Bitter Orange Sauce:
900 g (2 lb) Seville oranges, or tangy clementines
10 ml (2 tsp) arrowroot
icing sugar, to taste

Citrus Cream:
450 ml (¾ pint) double cream
juice of 1 small orange
juice of 1 small lemon
finely grated rind of ½ orange
finely grated rind of ½ lemon
25 ml (1 fl oz) Cointreau or Grand Marnier
icing sugar, to taste

To Decorate:
sifted cocoa powder, for dusting

Butter the base of a 20 cm (8 inch) loose-bottomed deep cake tin.

For the praline, spread the pistachios on a greased baking tray and toast lightly under the grill until browned. Place the sugar and 60 ml (4 tbsp) water in a heavy-based pan over a low heat and stir until dissolved. Continue to cook over a high heat until the syrup forms a golden brown caramel. Immediately pour over the pistachios, turning to coat evenly, then leave to cool and harden. When cool, break up the praline and work in a food processor until coarsely ground.

Mix the crushed biscuits with the melted butter and 125 g (4 oz) praline. Press onto the base of the cake tin and refrigerate for 30 minutes.

Whisk the egg yolks and sugar together in a bowl until light and creamy. Beat in the cream cheese, ground almonds, milk and cocoa powder until the mixture is smooth. In a clean bowl, whisk the egg whites until soft peaks form, then carefully fold into the chocolate mixture.

Spoon into the prepared tin and bake in a preheated oven at 170°C (325°F) mark 3 for 50 minutes, or until firm to the touch. Leave to cool in the tin.

To make the orange sauce, squeeze the juice from the oranges and strain through a sieve into a pan. Bring to the boil and boil until reduced by about half. Mix the arrowroot with 30 ml (2 tbsp) cold water and add to the sauce a little at a time, until slightly thickened. Allow to cool, then sweeten with icing sugar to taste.

For the citrus cream, whip the cream until soft peaks form, then whisk in the citrus juices and rinds until evenly incorporated. Add the liqueur and sweeten with icing sugar to taste.

To serve, remove cheesecake from tin and dust with cocoa powder, then cut into wedges. Serve on a 'pool' of orange sauce, with a spoonful of citrus cream.

Note: If preferred make individual cheesecakes in individual flan tins. Bake as above for about 40 minutes.

THE NORTH EAST

ASHLEY WILSON • MICHAEL DEACON • ALEXANDRA IVES

PANEL OF JUDGES

Anna del Conte • Mick Hucknall • Loyd Grossman

WINNER

ASHLEY WILSON'S MENU

STARTER

Wild Mushroom Consommé,
served with Olive Croûtons

"This was a phenomenal dish" **Anna del Conte**

MAIN COURSE

Venison with Black Pudding,
served with a Mushroom Sauce

Swede Purée

Parsnip Streamers

"The black pudding actually made the venison a lot more interesting...
it lent it a richness and a different sort of texture" **Loyd**

DESSERT

Hot Cherries and Lime Sherbet
in Pepper Tuile Baskets

"I think the pudding was just, just right" **Loyd**

Ashley Wilson from Sunderland is a vet in nearby Durham where
he looks after an interesting cross-section of family pets – from
Monty the python to Mabel the chinchilla! Ashley keeps himself
fit with regular games at the Durham squash club. He is also
a lover of fine wines.

WILD MUSHROOM CONSOMMÉ

20 g (¾ oz) dried mushrooms
500 ml (16 fl oz) chicken stock
1 egg white
15 ml (1 tbsp) Madeira
salt and freshly ground black pepper
15 ml (1 tbsp) black olive paste
15 ml (1 tbsp) extra-virgin olive oil
50 g (2 oz) ciabatta

Soak the dried mushrooms in 400 ml (14 fl oz) water for 30 minutes. (Measure 100 ml (3½ fl oz) of the soaking liquor and set aside for the main course sauce.) Combine the rest of the liquor and the mushrooms with the stock in a saucepan. Add the egg white and heat gently, whisking continuously, with a wire whisk, until a thick froth forms on the surface. Reduce the heat and simmer very gently for 1 hour.

Strain the consommé through a double layer of muslin, then strain again through the egg foam. Add the Madeira, reheat the consommé and check the seasoning.

Mix the olive paste with the olive oil. Cut the ciabatta into small cubes and toss them in the olive mixture. Spread out on a baking sheet and bake in a preheated oven at 190°C (370°F) mark 5 for 8 minutes.

Divide the consommé between warmed soup bowls and scatter a few croûtons onto each serving.

VENISON WITH BLACK PUDDING AND A MUSHROOM SAUCE

4 venison fillets, each about 150 g (5 oz)
30 ml (2 tbsp) olive oil

Marinade:
150 ml (¼ pint) olive oil
150 ml (¼ pint) red wine
30 ml (2 tbsp) balsamic vinegar
1 celery stalk, chopped
20 juniper berries, crushed
salt and freshly ground black pepper

Mushroom Sauce:
15 ml (1 tbsp) demerara sugar
15 ml (1 tbsp) balsamic vinegar
475 ml (15 fl oz) chicken stock
100 ml (3½ fl oz) dried mushroom soaking
  liquor (reserved from starter)
10 ml (2 tsp) redcurrant jelly

Black Pudding Purée:
225 g (8 oz) black pudding
30 ml (2 tbsp) olive oil
50 ml (2 fl oz) chicken stock (approximately)

Mix all the marinade ingredients together in a shallow dish. Add the venison fillets, cover and leave to marinate in the refrigerator for 2-4 hours.

Meanwhile, make the sauce. Melt the sugar in a small heavy-based saucepan over a low heat, then continue to cook over a medium heat without stirring until caramelised. Carefully add the balsamic vinegar and about 30 ml (2 tbsp) of the stock (protect your hand with a cloth as the mixture will boil and spurt furiously). Continue heating and stirring until the caramel has dissolved; if necessary, stubborn pieces of caramel can be removed with a slotted spoon and discarded. Add the rest of the stock, the mushroom liquor and the redcurrant jelly. Bring to the boil and reduce to approximately 300 ml (½ pint). Strain through a fine sieve and season with salt and pepper to taste.

Steam the black pudding for 10 minutes, then transfer to a food processor or blender with the olive oil. Process, adding sufficient stock to make a fairly smooth purée (the purée will not be perfectly smooth but should be processed long enough to be reasonably so).

Heat the olive oil in a heavy-based frying pan, add the venison fillets and fry over a medium-high heat for 2 minutes on each of the four sides. Wrap in foil and leave to rest in a warm place for 5-10 minutes. Reheat the sauce and the black pudding purée. Slice each venison fillet into 6 or 8 pieces. Arrange the venison slices on a bed of swede purée, fanned out and sandwiched with a little of the black pudding. Serve topped with parsnip streamers and surrounded by a pool of mushroom sauce.

SWEDE PURÉE

100 g (3½ oz) butter
200 g (7 oz) onions, coarsely chopped
650 g (1½ lb) swede
250 ml (8 fl oz) chicken stock
salt and freshly ground black pepper

Melt the butter in a heavy-based saucepan, add the onions and cook gently until soft. Add the swede and the stock and bring to the boil. Turn the heat down to very low and cover the pan with a sheet of greaseproof paper and a tight-fitting lid. Cook for 30 minutes. Transfer the contents of the pan to a blender or food processor and work until smooth. Season with salt and pepper to taste.

PARSNIPS STREAMERS

4 large parsnips, peeled
oil for deep-frying
salt and freshly ground black pepper

Using a swivel vegetable peeler, pare the parsnips into long thin strips. Heat the oil in a deep-fryer or deep saucepan to 180°C (350°F), or until a cube of bread dropped into the oil turns golden brown in 1 minute. Deep-fry the parsnip strips in batches for about 5 minutes until crisp and brown. Drain on kitchen paper and keep warm while frying the rest. Season with a little salt and pepper and serve piping hot.

LIME SHERBET WITH HOT CHERRIES

Lime Sherbet:
3 limes
7.5 ml (1½ tsp) lemon juice
85 g (3 oz) caster sugar
20 ml (4 tsp) golden syrup
280 ml (½ pint) milk
140 ml (¼ pint) single cream

Hot Cherries:
680 g (1 lb 8 oz) jar pitted morello cherries
  in syrup
100 g (3½ oz) sugar
5 ml (1 tsp) lemon juice
30 ml (2 tbsp) kirsch

To Serve:
Pepper Tuile Baskets (see right)

Drain the cherries. Purée 225 g (8 oz) of them and pass through a sieve into a small saucepan. Add the sugar, 15 ml (1 tbsp) water and the lemon juice. Bring to the boil, reduce the heat and cook until reduced to approximately 150 ml (¼ pint). Add the rest of the cherries and the kirsch and heat through.

To make the lime sherbet, squeeze the juice from the limes and pour it into a shallow freezerproof dish. Add the lemon juice. Place in the freezer for about 30 minutes until frozen to a slushy consistency.

Meanwhile, pare the zest from two of the limes in fine shreds and put it in a saucepan. Cover with cold water, bring to the boil and drain. Cover the zest with fresh cold water, bring to the boil and simmer for 20 minutes, then drain.

Melt the syrup in a little of the milk. Combine all the ingredients and churn in an ice-cream maker for about 20 minutes. Transfer to the freezer, removing the sherbet 5 minutes before serving. Serve the sherbet in the pepper tuile baskets, accompanied by the hot cherries.

PEPPER TUILE BASKETS

1 egg white (size 3)
50 g (2 oz) caster sugar
pinch of salt
30 g (1 oz) plain flour
30 g (1 oz) unsalted butter, melted
freshly ground black pepper

In a bowl, whisk the egg white with the sugar, salt and 10 ml (2 tsp) water until well blended. Stir in the flour and melted butter until smooth. Season generously with black pepper to taste (I use about 5 or 6 turns of the pepper mill).

Spread the batter thinly to form 5 circles, each about 12 cm (5 inches) in diameter on a baking tray lined with non-stick baking parchment. Bake in a preheated oven at 200°C (400°F) mark 6 for 5 to 6 minutes until the edges are golden.

As soon as the tuiles are removed from the oven, lift from the baking sheet, using a fish slice, and mould each one over an upturned greased teacup to form a basket. If the tuiles become too cool to mould easily, return them to the oven for about 30 seconds to soften. When cool and firm, remove the tuile baskets from the teacups.

Note: I always make an extra basket in case of a breakage when shaping the biscuits.

THE NORTH EAST

ASHLEY WILSON • MICHAEL DEACON • ALEXANDRA IVES

PANEL OF JUDGES
Anna del Conte • Mick Hucknall • Loyd Grossman

MICHAEL DEACON'S MENU

STARTER

*Grilled Red Mullet on Stir-fried Vegetables
with a Cream Sauce*

"The red mullet was delicious" **Loyd**

MAIN COURSE

Medallions of Venison in a Rich Red Wine Sauce

Cabbage with Garlic and Juniper

Quenelles of Sweet Potato and Parsnip

"The second course was excellent" **Mick Hucknall**

DESSERT

Vanilla Bavarois with Orange and Grand Marnier Sauce

Viennese Biscuits

"The pudding was perfection. Not only pretty but
very, very good" **Anna del Conte**

M ichael Deacon from Leeds is a systems analyst with the Halifax Building Society. He is currently responsible for setting up computer systems in their new dealing room. To get away from it all Michael has recently taken up the Triathlon which involves cycling, swimming and running long distances in quick succession. In slightly quieter moments the Deacon family are regulars at Eureka, the Children's Museum in Halifax.

Grilled Red Mullet on Stir-fried Vegetables with a Cream Sauce

4 red mullet, each 200-225 g (7-8 oz)

Stir Fry:
30 ml (2 tbsp) sesame oil
2 cloves garlic, finely chopped
25 g (1 oz) fresh root ginger, peeled and cut into julienne
50 g (2 oz) carrot, cut into julienne
50 g (2 oz) red pepper, cored, seeded and cut into julienne
50 g (2 oz) yellow pepper, cored, seeded and cut into julienne
50 g (2 oz) spring onions, sliced
50 g (2 oz) radish, sliced
50 g (2 oz) mooli, peeled and cut into julienne
50 g (2 oz) Chinese leaves or cabbage, shredded
125 g (4 oz) bean sprouts

Sauce:
150 ml (¼ pint) dry white wine
150 ml (¼ pint) fish stock
150 ml (¼ pint) double cream
25 g (1 oz) butter, diced
salt and freshly ground black pepper

Cut the head and fins off the red mullet, leaving on the tails. Using a knife, remove the scales working from the tail towards the head. Take the fillets off the bone leaving the skin on. Carefully remove any remaining bones from the centre of the fillets. Rinse the fish and set aside in a cool place.

To make the fish stock for the sauce, put the head and bones into a pan and cover with 300 ml (½ pint) water. Bring to the boil and skim the surface. Simmer gently for 15-20 minutes, skimming as necessary, until reduced to about 150 ml (¼ pint). Strain the stock through a fine sieve and set aside.

Preheat the grill to high. Meanwhile, heat the sesame oil in a wok or large pan until hot. Add the garlic and ginger and stir for a few seconds, then add the remaining vegetables and stir-fry for 2-3 minutes. Remove from the wok and keep warm.

To make the sauce, add the wine to the wok and reduce by two thirds, then add the fish stock and boil until reduced by half. Add the double cream, bring to the boil then simmer for 2 minutes.

Meanwhile, grill the mullet skin-side up for 2-3 minutes until the skins begin to turn golden; this is sufficient to cook the fillets through without turning them.

To finish the sauce, remove from the heat and add the butter a little at a time, swirling it into the sauce until it is incorporated and the sauce is shiny. Check the seasoning.

To serve, pile the stir-fried vegetables in the centre of warmed serving plates. Arrange the mullet skin-side up and slightly overlapping on top. Surround with the sauce and serve at once.

MEDALLIONS OF VENISON IN A RICH RED WINE SAUCE

This dish is better if the venison is allowed to marinate for 2-3 days. If time is short you can use roe deer to avoid marinating. Ask your butcher to fillet the saddle and chop the bones into small pieces.

575 g (1¼ lb) venison fillet (plus the bones
  from the saddle)
salt and freshly ground black pepper
a little oil, for cooking

Marinade:
30 ml (2 tbsp) olive oil
50 g (2 oz) shallots, finely chopped
50 g (2 oz) carrots, diced
125 g (4 oz) celery, diced
50 g (2 oz) mushrooms, diced
45 ml (3 tbsp) red wine vinegar
500 ml (16 fl oz) full-bodied red wine
5 ml (1 tsp) juniper berries
small bunch of thyme sprigs
1 bay leaf
2 cloves garlic, finely chopped

Sauce:
30 ml (2 tbsp) dark treacle or molasses
60 ml (4 tbsp) light soy sauce

To Garnish:
thyme sprigs

To prepare the marinade, heat the oil in a heavy-based pan until hot, then brown the venison bones. Transfer to a large bowl. Add the shallots, carrots, celery and mushrooms to the pan and cook until golden. Deglaze the pan with the vinegar, transfer to the bowl and allow to cool. Cut the venison into 4 equal portions and add to the bowl, with the wine, juniper berries, thyme, bay leaf and garlic. Leave to marinate in the refrigerator for up to 3 days.

Remove the venison from the marinade, pat dry and set aside in a cool place. Transfer the marinade (including the bones and vegetables) to a pan, bring to the boil and reduce by half. Stir in the treacle or molasses, 200 ml (7 fl oz) water and the soy sauce. Simmer for 1 hour or until reduce to a shiny sauce-like consistency.

About 20 minutes before the sauce has finished reducing, cut the venison into medallions, about 2.5 cm (1 inch) thick. Flatten slightly with the palm of your hand and season with salt and pepper. Heat a thin film of oil in a frying pan until very hot, add the medallions and seal on each side. Transfer to a lightly oiled baking tray then roast in a preheated oven at 190°C (375°F) mark 5 for about 5 minutes; keep warm.

Strain the sauce through a fine sieve and season with pepper to taste.

To serve, place some cabbage to one side of each warmed serving plate. Arrange the venison medallions on the cabbage and pour the sauce over them and around the plate. Place the quenelles of sweet potato and parsnip opposite and garnish with a sprig of thyme.

CABBAGE WITH GARLIC AND JUNIPER

450 g (1 lb) Savoy cabbage, cored and shred-
ded
30 ml (2 tbsp) olive oil
75 g (3 oz) onion, very finely sliced
1 clove garlic, finely chopped
6 juniper berries
salt and freshly ground black pepper

Heat the olive oil in a large pan, add the onion and fry until golden. Meanwhile crush the juniper berries using a pestle and mortar (or with the back of a spoon on a flat surface). Add the juniper berries and garlic to the onion and fry for about 1 minute. Add the cabbage and stir until well coated with the oil. Season with salt and pepper, then cover and cook for about 10 minutes, stirring occasionally.

QUENELLES OF SWEET POTATO AND PARSNIP

700 g (1½ lb) sweet potatoes (preferably
orange-fleshed), peeled
450 g (1 lb) parsnips, peeled
knob of butter
salt and freshly ground black pepper

Cut the potatoes and parsnip into even-sized pieces and steam or cook separately in boiling water until tender; drain thoroughly. Purée the sweet potatoes until smooth and season with salt and pepper to taste. Purée the parsnips, adding a knob of butter and seasoning. Shape the vegetable purée into quenelles by scooping the purée from one tablespoon to another until a quenelle is formed. Serve piping hot.

Note: For optimum results, use a food mill or masher to purée the vegetables, rather than a food processor.

VANILLA BAVAROIS WITH ORANGE AND GRAND MARNIER SAUCE

Orange Jelly:

1 gelatine leaf
40 g (1½ oz) caster sugar
150 ml (¼ pint) fresh orange juice

Bavarois:

3 gelatine leaves
5 egg yolks
50 g (2 oz) caster sugar
250 ml (8 fl oz) milk
1 vanilla pod or vanilla extract
300 ml (½ pint) whipping cream

Orange and Grand Marnier Sauce:

75 g (3 oz) caster sugar
275 ml (9 fl oz) fresh orange juice
finely pared zest of 1 orange, shredded
5 ml (1 tsp) arrowroot, mixed with a little
   water
30 ml (2 tbsp) Grand Marnier

To make the jelly, soak the gelatine leaf in cold water to cover. Meanwhile dissolve the sugar in the orange juice in a pan over a low heat. Bring to the boil, then remove from the heat. Squeeze excess water from the gelatine leaf, then add it to the pan and stir until dissolved. Pour the jelly into 4 dariole moulds to a depth of about 1 cm (½ inch). Place in the refrigerator until set.

To make the bavarois, soak the gelatine leaves in cold water to cover. Beat the egg yolks and sugar together in a bowl until thick and creamy. Put the milk and vanilla pod in a saucepan and bring to the boil. Remove from the heat and take out the vanilla pod. Add the milk to the egg and sugar mixture, stirring constantly, then return to the pan. Stir over a low heat until the custard thickens enough to coat the back of a spoon; do not allow to boil. Squeeze excess water from the gelatine, then add to the

warm custard off the heat, stirring to dissolve.

Pour the custard into a bowl set over ice and leave to cool, stirring occasionally, until it begins to set around the edge. Lightly whip the cream and fold into the mixture. Pour over the jelly to fill the dariole moulds. Refrigerate until set.

To make the sauce, place the sugar and orange juice in a pan with the orange zest strips and bring to the boil. Stir in the arrowroot and cook, stirring, for 1 minute to thicken the sauce to a syrupy consistency. Pour into a jug and allow to cool. Just before serving, stir in the Grand Marnier.

To serve, dip the moulds in warm water for a few seconds, then run a knife around the edge. Invert each bavarois on to the centre of a serving plate. Pour the sauce around and serve with the Viennese biscuits.

VIENNESE BISCUITS

125 g (4 oz) butter, well softened
25 g (1 oz) icing sugar, sifted
150 g (5 oz) plain flour, sifted
icing sugar, for dredging

Cream the butter and icing sugar together in a bowl until very soft and light. Stir in the flour and mix well. Put the mixture into a piping bag fitted with a large star nozzle and pipe small rosettes onto a greased baking tray. Chill in the refrigerator for about 15 minutes, then bake in a preheated oven at 190°C (375°F) mark 5 for about 10 minutes until they are just beginning to turn golden brown. Cool on a wire rack. Dredge with icing sugar to serve.

Note: If the butter is not very soft the mixture will be too stiff to pipe. A few drops of milk can be added if necessary.

THE NORTH EAST

ASHLEY WILSON • MICHAEL DEACON • ALEXANDRA IVES

PANEL OF JUDGES
Anna del Conte • Mick Hucknall • Loyd Grossman

ALEXANDRA IVES' MENU

STARTER

Miniature Herbed Yorkshire Puddings
filled with a Medley of Mushrooms

"I loved the idea" **Loyd**

MAIN COURSE

Mousseline of Sea Trout
with a Coriander Hollandaise

Courgettes en Barque

"The mousseline itself was perfect" **Anna del Conte**

DESSERT

Champagne and Apple Sorbet
with a Cassis Sauce

"Presentation was marvellous. The sauce was
very good" **Anna del Conte**

Alexandra Ives has recently moved in to her new home in
Brompton, North Yorkshire, where she trained as a banker.
Renovating her newly acquired property takes up much
of Alexandra's spare time. Her leisure pursuits also include
clay pigeon shooting and quad bikes.

MINIATURE HERBED YORKSHIRE PUDDINGS FILLED WITH A MEDLEY OF MUSHROOMS

Yorkshire Puddings:
65 g (2½ oz) strong plain flour
1 egg
75 ml (5 tbsp) semi-skimmed milk
75 ml (5 tbsp) water
salt and freshly ground black pepper
10 ml (2 tsp) chopped parsley
10 ml (2 tsp) chopped mint
goose fat or white vegetable fat, for greasing

Medley of Mushrooms:
25 g (1 oz) butter
15 ml (1 tbsp) sesame oil
3 shallots, finely chopped
225 g (8 oz) mixed mushrooms (preferably shiitake and oyster or chestnut), sliced
dash of dry sherry
90 ml (3 fl oz) single cream

To Garnish:
mint or parsley sprigs

Sift the flour into a bowl and make a well in the centre. Add the eggs, milk and water to the well. Whisk until thoroughly combined, then season with salt and pepper and add the chopped herbs. Leave to stand for at least 2 minutes. Grease a 12-hole mini-muffin tin with goose fat and place in a very hot oven at 230°C (450°F) mark 8 for 5-6 minutes. Pour the mixture into the tins almost to the top and cook in the oven for about 15 minutes until well risen and golden.

Meanwhile, heat the butter and sesame oil in a pan. Add the shallots and sweat gently until softened. Add the mushrooms and sauté briefly. Add a dash of sherry and pour in the cream. Allow to bubble to thicken slightly until the alcohol has evaporated and the sauce is pale brown in colour. Season with salt and pepper to taste.

Once the Yorkshire puddings are cooked, remove from the oven and split them open. Place on warmed serving plates and fill with the mushrooms. Surround with the sauce and garnish with herbs. Serve at once.

MOUSSELINE OF SEA TROUT WITH A CORIANDER HOLLANDAISE

575 g (2¼ lb) piece sea trout (middle-cut)
2-3 egg whites
300 ml (½ pint) double cream
squeeze of lime juice
squeeze of fresh ginger sauce
1 clove garlic, crushed
salt and freshly ground pepper

Coriander Hollandaise:
450 ml (¾ pint) fish stock (see below)
200 g (7 oz) unsalted butter
5 egg yolks
squeeze of lemon juice (optional)
30 ml (2 tbsp) chopped coriander

To Garnish:
deep-fried leek strips (optional)

Skin and bone the sea trout, reserving the trimmings (to make a stock for the hollandaise). Lay the fillet out on a board and, using a suitable pastry cutter, cut 8 rounds to fit 4 ramekin dishes. Season four of the rounds lightly with salt and pepper and use to line the base of the buttered ramekin dishes. Place in the refrigerator, with the other rounds.

Put the rest of the sea trout in a food processor and process briefly until just smooth. With the machine running, gradually add the egg whites until the mixture is firm and smooth, then slowly add the cream. (If you have time, put the mixture in a bowl over a larger bowl of crushed ice before beating in the cream, a quarter at a time, refrigerating the mousseline for 15 minutes between each addition.) Add the lime juice, ginger juice, garlic and seasoning to taste. Chill in the refrigerator for at least 20 minutes.

Meanwhile, make the coriander hollandaise. Boil the fish stock to reduce down to about 15 ml (1 tbsp) liquid. Melt the butter in a pan and heat until it is

bubbling. Whizz the egg yolks in a food processor, then add the reduced stock. With the machine running, gradually add the melted butter. Season with salt and pepper to taste. Stir in the coriander, and lemon juice if desired.

Spoon the chilled mousseline into the ramekins, dividing it equally between them. Smooth the surface and top with the other fish rounds. Cover each ramekin with a disc of buttered greaseproof paper and stand the dishes in a bain-marie (roasting tin containing enough boiling water to come halfway up the sides of the dishes). Bake in a preheated oven at 180°C (350°F) mark 4 for 10-12 minutes or until springy to the touch.

Run a knife around the edge of each mousseline and turn out onto individual serving dishes. Blot off any cooking juices with kitchen paper. Surround with the coriander hollandaise and garnish with thin strips of deep-fried leeks if desired. Serve at once, with the accompaniments.

Fish Stock: Put the fish trimmings in a large saucepan with 1 small onion or leek, halved; 1 carrot; 1 bay leaf and 1 small wine glass of dry white wine. Add 600 ml (1 pint) water and bring to the boil. Skim, then simmer, uncovered, for 20 minutes. Strain through a fine sieve.

COURGETTES EN BARQUE

*4 plump courgettes, each 12 cm (5 inches)
long, trimmed*

Carrot Purée:
*350 g (12 oz) carrots, peeled and thinly
sliced
salt and freshly ground black pepper
1.25 ml (¼ tsp) freshly grated nutmeg
knob of butter, to taste*

To make the 'courgette boats', cut the
courgettes lengthwise into 1 cm (½ inch)
thick slices, discarding the outer curved
edges. Blanch in boiling water for
1 minute, then refresh in cold water and
pat dry. Using a sharp knife, make an
incision along the green (skin) side of
each slice, leaving 1 cm (½ inch) uncut at
each end.

Steam the carrots or cook in boiling
water until tender. Drain and purée in a
blender or using a food mill until
smooth. Season with salt, pepper and
nutmeg, and add butter to taste.

Place the courgettes on a baking sheet,
opening them up to form little boats. Fill
with the carrot purée and reheat in a
moderate oven at 180°C (350°F) mark 4
just before serving.

CHAMPAGNE AND APPLE SORBET WITH A CASSIS SAUCE

*500 g (1 lb 2 oz) apples
200 g (7 oz) sugar
⅓ bottle Champagne
juice of 2 lemons
300 ml (½ pint) double cream*

Cassis Sauce:
*225 g (8 oz) blackcurrants
125 ml (4 fl oz) crème de cassis liqueur
175 g (6 oz) caster sugar (approximately)*

Peel, quarter and core the apples. Place
in a heavy-based pan with about 60 ml
(4 tbsp) water and cook, stirring occasionally, until soft. Pass through a sieve
into a bowl. Allow to cool. You should
have 225 g (8 oz) apple purée.

Dissolve the sugar in 350 ml (12 fl oz)
water in a heavy-based saucepan over a
low heat. Bring slowly to the boil, then
increase the heat and boil for about
2 minutes until a light syrup is obtained.
Remove the syrup from the heat and
leave to cool.

Stir the sugar syrup, Champagne,
lemon juice and cream into the apple
purée. Pour into the ice-cream maker and
churn until firm.

Meanwhile, place the ingredients for
the sauce in a heavy-based pan. Bring to
a simmer and cook until reduced to the
desired consistency. Taste and add a little
more sugar if desired. Pass through a
sieve if a smooth sauce is preferred.

Serve the sorbet scooped into individual glass bowls, accompanied by the
cassis sauce.

Note: If you do not have an ice-cream
maker, freeze the sorbet in a suitable
container, whisking 2-3 times during
freezing to break down the ice crystals
and ensure a smooth-textured result.

LONDON

HOLLY SCHADE • ABIGAIL BARLOW • JENNY REES

PANEL OF JUDGES

Nick Nairn • Honor Blackman • Loyd Grossman

WINNER

HOLLY SCHADE'S MENU

STARTER

Spicy Butternut Squash and Apple Soup

"Fabulous. The soup was wonderful" **Nick Nairn**

MAIN COURSE

Veal Medallions
with Onion Marmalade

Sage Tagliatelle

French Beans

"The veal was very nice... I liked the onion marmalade with it...
and the tagliatelle" **Nick Nairn**

DESSERT

Chocolate Pecan Pie,
served with Vanilla Ice Cream

"I think it was sensational, sensational" **Nick Nairn**

Holly Schade left her roots in Concorde, New Hampshire, USA, to live in Kensington, London. A former member of the Princeton track team, Holly is a great keep-fit enthusiast and spends much of her time at the Riverside Club in the gym, playing tennis, swimming or enjoying activities with her daughter Katherine. Holly is also a talented musician, and plays the violin.

SPICY BUTTERNUT SQUASH AND APPLE SOUP

40 g (1½ oz) butter
1 onion, finely chopped
1 large clove garlic, crushed
700 g (1½ lb) butternut squash, peeled,
* seeded and cut into chunks*
3 Granny Smith apples, peeled, cored and
* cut into chunks*
750 ml (1 ¼ pints) chicken stock
5-10 ml (1-2 tsp) ground cumin
salt and freshly ground black pepper
60 ml (4 tbsp) crème fraîche

To Garnish:
1 red apple, quartered, cored and sliced

Melt the butter in a heavy-based saucepan, add the onion and sauté until soft. Add the garlic and sauté for a further 2 minutes. Add the squash, apple and chicken stock. Simmer for about 15 minutes, until the squash is tender. Stir in the cumin and salt and pepper to taste.

Using a blender or food processor, purée the soup in batches until smooth, transforming the puréed soup to a clean saucepan. Heat through, then divide between warmed soup bowls. Add a spoonful of crème fraîche to each portion and garnish with the apple slices.

Veal Medallions with Onion Marmalade

4 onions, sliced
salt and freshly ground black pepper
750 ml (1¼ pints) chicken stock
22 ml (1½ tbsp) red wine vinegar
350 ml (12 fl oz) double cream
8 veal medallions, each about 75 g (3 oz)
flour, for dusting
30 ml (2 tbsp) sunflower oil
50 g (2 oz) butter
250 ml (8 fl oz) port

To Garnish:
sage leaves

Put the onions in a medium saucepan and season with salt and pepper. Add 500 ml (16 fl oz) of the chicken stock and the vinegar. Cook, covered, over a moderate heat for about 15 minutes until the liquid is almost totally evaporated.

In a separate small pan, bring the cream to the boil and boil steadily to reduce to 60-75 ml (4-5 tbsp). Add the cream to the onions and bring back to the boil. Check the seasoning and remove from the heat.

Season the veal with salt and pepper and dust all over with flour. Heat the oil and half of the butter in a large heavy-based frying pan. Add the veal and sauté for 3-4 minutes on each side until browned, but still pink inside. Transfer to a warmed platter and keep warm.

Pour off any remaining fat from the pan, then add the port to deglaze, scraping up any sediment from the base of the pan. Add the remaining chicken stock, bring to the boil and boil to reduce to 60-75 ml (4-5 tbsp). Gradually whisk in the remaining 25 g (1 oz) butter, a piece at a time, to yield a smooth glossy sauce.

To serve, gently reheat the onions and spoon a portion onto each warmed serving plate. Top with the veal and spoon on the sauce. Garnish with sage and serve with the tagliatelle and French beans.

Sage Tagliatelle

To make this tagliatelle you will need to use a pasta machine. For optimum results use Italian "00" flour but, if unavailable, plain flour can be substituted.

310 g (10½ oz) Italian "00" flour
pinch of salt
3 eggs (size 2)
3 drops of olive oil
15 ml (1 tbsp) finely chopped sage

To Serve:
butter, to taste
sage leaves, to garnish

To make the pasta dough, put the flour, salt, eggs, olive oil and sage in a food processor and process for about 30 seconds or until the dough forms a ball. Flatten the ball slightly with your hands, wrap in cling film and leave to rest in the refrigerator for 30 minutes.

Cut off about one quarter of the dough and rewrap the remainder. Flatten the piece and shape into a rectangle. Pass it through the pasta machine on its widest setting. Fold the dough and pass through the machine repeatedly, narrowing the setting by one notch each time until it passes through the second to last notch. Repeat with the remaining dough, then fit the tagliatelle attachment. Pass the pasta sheets through to cut the tagliatelle. Lay on clean tea-towels and leave to dry slightly, for about 5 minutes, before cooking.

Cook the tagliatelle in a large pan of boiling salted water for about 2 minutes until *al dente* (tender but firm to the bite). Drain and toss with butter to taste. Garnish with sage leaves.

CHOCOLATE PECAN PIE

Pastry:

185 g (6½ oz) plain flour
2.5 ml (½ tsp) salt
5 ml (1 tsp) caster sugar
65 g (2½ oz) butter
25 g (1 oz) white vegetable shortening, in pieces
(2½-3 tbsp) iced water

Filling:

50 g (2 oz) plain chocolate, in pieces
50 g (2 oz) butter
4 eggs (size 1)
250 ml (8 fl oz) maple syrup
225 g (8 oz) caster sugar
5 ml (1 tsp) vanilla essence
350 g (12 oz) shelled pecan nuts, roughly chopped

To make the pastry, put the flour, salt, sugar, butter and vegetable shortening in a food processor. Process, using the pulse button, until the mixture begins to resemble breadcrumbs; do not over-mix. Transfer the mixture to a bowl and sprinkle over 40 ml (2½ tbsp) iced water. Toss with a fork, sprinkling in a little more iced water as necessary until the mixture begins to stick together. Working quickly, draw the dough together with your hands and form into a ball.

Roll out the pastry on a lightly floured surface and use to line a 23 cm (9 inch) fluted flan tin. Trim and crimp the edges. Chill in the refrigerator for 30 minutes.

Meanwhile, prepare the filling. Put the chocolate and butter in a bowl and melt together in the microwave on MEDIUM (or over a pan of simmering water). Stir until smooth, then set aside to cool.

Put the eggs, maple syrup, sugar and vanilla essence in a mixing bowl and beat until well combined. Stir in the chocolate mixture, then fold in the nuts. Pour into the chilled pastry case and bake in the middle of a preheated oven at 190°C (375°F) mark 5 for 50-60 minutes, or until a skewer inserted into the centre comes out only slightly fudgy. Serve warm, with the ice cream.

VANILLA ICE CREAM

300 ml (½ pint) double cream
200 ml (7 fl oz) semi-skimmed milk
1 vanilla pod
2.5 ml (½ tsp) vanilla essence
4 egg yolks (size 1)
125 g (4 oz) caster sugar

Pour the cream and milk into a saucepan. Scrape the seeds from the vanilla pod into the liquid and add the vanilla essence. Slowly bring the mixture just to the boil. Meanwhile, beat the egg yolks and sugar together in a bowl until well blended. Slowly add the hot liquid, stirring constantly.

Return to the pan and stir over a low heat until the custard is thick enough to lightly coat the back of the wooden spoon; do not boil or it will curdle. Strain into a clean bowl and leave to cool. Transfer to an ice-cream maker and churn, according to the manufacturer's instructions, until firm. Serve with the pecan pie.

Note: If you do not have an ice-cream maker, freeze the ice cream in a suitable container, whisking 2-3 times during freezing to break down the ice crystals and ensure a smooth-textured result.

LONDON

HOLLY SCHADE • ABIGAIL BARLOW • JENNY REES

PANEL OF JUDGES

Nick Nairn • Honor Blackman • Loyd Grossman

ABIGAIL BARLOW'S MENU

STARTER

Smoked Mushroom and Chilli Tamales
with Avocado and Tequila Salsa

"It looked wonderful" **Nick Nairn**

MAIN COURSE

Seared Tuna Fillets
with a Slow-cooked Tomato Sauce

Potato and Beetroot Galette

Wilted Greens with Black Sesame Seeds

"The tuna was wonderful... beautifully cooked...
and the beetroot worked very well with it" **Nick Nairn**

DESSERT

Hot Strawberry Soufflé with Passion Fruit Purée

Shortbread Biscuits

"Yummy. It was really delicious I thought" **Honor Blackman**

A bigail Barlow lives in Fulham, in West London, and works with a leading wine importer. Being something of an artist, one of Abigail's responsibilities is designing the company's labels. In her leisure time, Abigail's creative flair is turned to designing and constructing stained glass windows. Her latest obsession, however, is golf and she is off to the driving range at every opportunity.

SMOKED MUSHROOM AND CHILLI TAMALES WITH AVOCADO AND TEQUILA SALSA

For this Mexican-style starter, you will need to obtain a few special ingredients from a Mexican food supplier.

50 g (2 oz) butter
225 g (8 oz) smoked mushrooms, chopped
15 ml (1 tbsp) chopped coriander
2 cloves roasted garlic, peeled (see note)
salt and freshly ground black pepper
1 smoked chilli, finely chopped
30 ml (2 tbsp) masa harina (see note)
125 g (4 oz) Monterey Jack cheese, grated
150 ml (¼ pint) vegetable stock (approximately)
8 large dried corn husks, pre-soaked in hot water

Avocado and Tequila Salsa:
1 green pepper, cored, seeded and finely chopped
1 avocado, peeled, stoned and chopped
juice of 2 limes
½ red onion, finely chopped
1 green chilli, finely chopped
15 ml (1 tbsp) chopped coriander
15 ml (1 tbsp) tequila
30 ml (2 tbsp) olive oil

First prepare the salsa. Combine all of the ingredients in a bowl and toss gently to mix. Cover and leave to stand for at least 1 hour.

Heat the butter in a frying pan, add the smoked mushrooms and fry gently until cooked. Allow to cool slightly, then transfer to a food processor and process on a very low speed until coarsely chopped. Transfer to a large mixing bowl and add the coriander, garlic, salt and pepper, chilli, masa harina and cheese. Stir well. Add the vegetable stock, a little at a time, until a soft dough is formed. You may not need to add all of the stock.

Open out a corn husk and place a dessertspoon of the dough in the centre. Roll to enclose the filling and form a cracker shape. Use extra thin pieces of husk to tie the ends together, or use string if preferred. Repeat with the rest of the corn husks. Place in a steamer and steam for 25 minutes. Serve the tamales with the salsa.

Note: Masa harina is a special type of maize flour. You should be able to obtain masa harina and dried corn husks from Mexican food suppliers.

For the roasted garlic, wrap the garlic cloves in foil and bake in a moderate oven for 20 minutes. For a milder flavoured salsa, remove the seeds from the chilli.

SEARED TUNA FILLETS WITH A SLOW-COOKED TOMATO SAUCE

4 pieces fresh tuna fillet, each about 125 g
(4 oz) and 1 cm (½ inch) thick
4 large basil leaves, torn
15 ml (1 tbsp) olive oil

Tomato Sauce:
450 g (1 lb) plum tomatoes
15 ml (1 tbsp) olive oil
5 ml (1 tsp) sugar
2 cloves roasted garlic (from the ½ head –
see below)

To Garnish:
basil leaves
½ head garlic, roasted (see note)

Place the tuna fillets in a shallow dish, sprinkle with the torn basil leaves and olive oil and turn to coat. Cover and leave to marinate in the refrigerator for about 2 hours.

Meanwhile, make the tomato sauce. Immerse the tomatoes in a bowl of boiling water for 30 seconds, then remove and peel away the skins. Deseed and chop the tomato flesh. Heat the olive oil in a large pan. Add the chopped tomatoes and sugar and cook for 2-3 minutes. Reduce the heat and cook very gently for 40 minutes, stirring occasionally. Add the garlic and purée in a blender or food processor until smooth. Season with salt and pepper to taste.

To cook the tuna, preheat a griddle or heavy-based frying pan over a high heat for 3-4 minutes (without any oil) until very hot. Place the tuna fillets on the griddle (or in the pan) and cook for 1-2 minutes each side.

To serve, place the tuna fillets on the potato and beetroot galettes and top with the tomato sauce. Garnish with basil and roasted garlic. Serve with the wilted greens.

Note: To roast the garlic, wrap the ½ head in foil and bake in a moderate oven for 30 minutes. It is essential to preheat the griddle until it is very hot otherwise the tuna will stick.

POTATO AND BEETROOT GALETTE

450 g (1 lb) raw beetroot
450 g (1 lb) purple potatoes
olive oil, for brushing

Rinse the beetroot and potatoes, but do not peel. Cut into 5 mm (¼ inch) thick slices, discarding the ends. Line a baking sheet with lightly oiled greaseproof paper. Arrange the beetroot and potato rounds alternately on the paper to form 4 circles, overlapping the slices. Brush with oil and bake in a preheated oven at 200°C (400°F) mark 6 for 30 minutes.

WILTED GREENS WITH BLACK SESAME SEEDS

450 g (1 lb) mixed leafy greens (eg spinach,
watercress, spring greens), stalks removed
and finely chopped
15 ml (1 tbsp) sesame oil
15 ml (1 tbsp) black sesame seeds

Heat the oil in a wok, add the sesame seeds and fry for 30 seconds, then add the greens and stir-fry for 2 minutes. Serve immediately.

HOT STRAWBERRY SOUFFLÉ WITH PASSION FRUIT PURÉE

375 g (13 oz) strawberries, hulled
5 egg whites
225 g (8 oz) sugar
15 ml (1 tbsp) cornflour
30 ml (2 tbsp) Cointreau or Grand Marnier

To Decorate:
4 passion fruit

Purée the strawberries in a blender or food processor, then pass through a sieve to remove the pips; set aside. Butter 4 individual 250 ml (8 fl oz) soufflé dishes and dust with caster sugar.

Whisk the egg whites in a bowl until stiff. Dissolve the sugar in 125 ml (4 fl oz) water in a saucepan over a low heat, then increase the heat and boil for 1 minute until the syrup thickens slightly. Pour the hot syrup onto the egg whites in a thin steady stream, whisking all the time, until thick and glossy. Continue to whisk for a further 2-3 minutes.

Beat in the cornflour, then carefully fold in the strawberry purée and liqueur. Divide the mixture between the prepared soufflé dishes and place in a preheated oven at 220°C (425°F) mark 7. Immediately lower the oven setting to 190°C (375°F) mark 5 and bake for 30 minutes.

Meanwhile cut the passion fruit in half and place one half on the side of each serving plate, with a few shortbread biscuits. Stand the cooked soufflés on the serving plates and scoop the pulp and seeds from the remaining passion fruit on top. Dust with icing sugar, if desired. Serve immediately.

SHORTBREAD BISCUITS

75 g (3 oz) plain flour
50 g (2 oz) butter
25 g (1 oz) caster sugar
few drops of vanilla extract

Sift the flour into a bowl and rub in the butter. Add the sugar and vanilla extract and work the ingredients together with your fingers to form a smooth dough.

Divide the dough into 4 equal pieces and lightly press each portion into a greased madeleine tin. Bake in a preheated oven at 190°C (375°F) mark 5 for 15-20 minutes. Leave to cool on a wire rack, then remove from tins, using a sharp knife to ease them out. Serve with the soufflé.

LONDON

HOLLY SCHADE • ABIGAIL BARLOW • JENNY REES

PANEL OF JUDGES

Nick Nairn • Honor Blackman • Loyd Grossman

JENNY REES' MENU

STARTER

Garlic Prawns on a Bed of Leeks

"I thought it was great... the prawns were very simple, but they had
a nice spicy, Oriental flavour to them" **Nick Nairn**

MAIN COURSE

Roasted Lamb with a Tamarind Sauce

*Ribbons of Courgette and Carrot
in a Lime and Coriander Glaze*

Potato Rösti

"The lamb was lovely... perfectly cooked. Everything came
together nicely" **Nick Nairn**

DESSERT

Peppered Pineapple, served in a Toffee Basket with Vanilla Ice Cream

"The peppered pineapple was wonderful" **Loyd**

Jenny Rees emigrated from Brisbane, Australia to Putney, London.
Being a typical Australian, Jenny loves the outdoor life: she
roller-skates by the nearby Thames and, with husband Ollie, flies
impressive kites on Parliament Hill. At home, Jenny relaxes by
practising her latest hobby, calligraphy.

GARLIC PRAWNS ON A BED OF LEEKS

1 large leek
12 raw king or tiger prawns
30 ml (2 tbsp) olive oil
1 clove garlic, crushed
15 ml (1 tbsp) Thai fish sauce (nam pla)
5 ml (1 tsp) brown sugar
5 ml (1 tsp) lightly crushed black pepper-
  corns

To Garnish:
chopped coriander leaves

Cut the leek into fine strips, about 3 cm (1¼ inches) long. Add to a pan of boiling salted water and cook briefly until just tender; drain well.

Shell the prawns, removing the heads but leaving the tails intact. Cut centrally along the back of each prawn and remove the dark intestinal vein. Flatten the prawns out slightly.

Heat the oil in a wok, add the prawns and garlic, and stir-fry for 2 minutes. Add the fish sauce, sugar and pepper-corns and stir-fry until the prawns are pink and just tender.

Arrange the leek julienne to form a nest on each warmed serving plate. Place 3 prawns in each nest, pour over the cooking juices and sprinkle with chopped coriander to serve.

ROASTED LAMB WITH A TAMARIND SAUCE

75 g (3 oz) tamarind pulp
15 ml (1 tbsp) olive oil
900 g (2 lb) piece boned lean lamb (leg, loin
  or chump)
450 ml (¾ pint) lamb stock
40 g (1½ oz) chilled butter, diced

Put the tamarind pulp in a bowl, pour on 250 ml (8 fl oz) boiling water and leave to soak for 15 minutes. Add the lamb and leave to marinate in a cool place for a few hours, or overnight if possible.

Remove the lamb from the marinade; pass the tamarind pulp through a sieve and reserve. Heat the oil in a heavy-based frying pan and brown the lamb on all sides. Transfer to a roasting tin and cook in a preheated oven at 230°C (450°F) mark 8 for 10 minutes. Transfer the meat to a warmed plate, cover and leave to rest for 5 minutes or so, before carving.

Meanwhile, deglaze the roasting tin with the lamb stock and tamarind pulp. Whisk in the butter, a piece at a time, until the sauce is shiny.

Carve the meat into slices and arrange on warmed serving plates on a pool of the sauce, with the accompaniments.

RIBBONS OF COURGETTE AND CARROTS IN A LIME AND CORIANDER GLAZE

450 g (1 lb) young carrots, scraped, topped
  and tailed
450 g (1 lb) courgettes, topped and tailed
salt
40 g (1½ oz) butter
10 ml (2 tsp) caster sugar
2.5 ml (½ tsp) ground coriander
finely pared zest of 1 lime, cut into fine juli-
  enne
22 ml (1½ tbsp) lime juice
15 ml (1 tbsp) chopped coriander leaves

Cut both the carrots and courgettes lengthwise into ribbons, using a swivel vegetable peeler.

Cook the carrots in boiling salted water until barely tender, about 4 minutes. Drain well and refresh under cold water. (The courgettes don't need pre-blanching.)

Just before serving, heat the butter in a wok or large frying pan until sizzling, then add the vegetables and sprinkle with the sugar, 2.5 ml (½ tsp) salt and the ground coriander. Toss over a high heat until glazed, then add the lime rind and juice. Toss over the heat for a few seconds longer. Serve scattered with the chopped coriander.

POTATO RÖSTI

2-3 baking potatoes
2 onions, finely chopped
40 g (1½ oz) butter
salt and freshly ground black pepper

Prick the potatoes with a fork and bake in a preheated oven at 200°C (400°F) mark 6 for 40 minutes until slightly softened, but not completely cooked through. Heat the butter in a pan, add the onions and sauté, without browning, for 5-7 minutes.

Leave the partially-baked potatoes in their skins until cool, then peel and grate coarsely. Stir in the onions and season with salt and pepper.

Spoon the mixture into mounds on a greased baking sheet. Bake at 200°C (400°F) mark 6 for 40 minutes or until crisp and golden.

PEPPERED PINEAPPLE IN TOFFEE BASKETS

125 g (4 oz) caster sugar
60 ml (2 fl oz) orange juice
15 ml (1 tbsp) lemon juice
90 ml (3 fl oz) crème de cacao
75 g (3 oz) unsalted butter
finely pared zest of ½ orange, shredded
½ pineapple or 1 small pineapple, about
    300 g (10 oz)
freshly ground black pepper

Toffee Baskets:
225 g (8 oz) granulated sugar
15 ml (1 tbsp) vinegar

To Serve:
Vanilla Ice Cream (see right)

First make the toffee baskets. Put the sugar, vinegar and 85 ml (3 fl oz) water in a small heavy-based pan over a low heat, stirring, until the sugar is dissolved, Bring to the boil and boil rapidly for 15 minutes without stirring until the syrup forms a golden caramel. Test by dropping a little of the mixture into cold water; it should form a brittle toffee. When ready, take off the heat and let cool for 1-2 minutes until it thickens slightly.

Oil the outside of 4 individual metal pudding basins. Turn the basins upside down and drizzle the toffee mixture backwards and forewards over them to form 4 baskets. Set aside until cool and set.

Meanwhile prepare the pineapple. Melt the caster sugar in a heavy-based pan over a low heat, then increase the heat to medium and cook to a golden brown caramel. Carefully add the orange juice, lemon juice and two thirds of the crème de cacao, protecting your hand with a cloth as the mixture will spurt furiously. Stir to dissolve the caramel and simmer gently to reduce slightly.

Melt 40 g (1½ oz) butter in a small pan, brown slightly, then stir into the sauce.

Blanch the orange zest shreds in boiling water for 1 minute, drain and add to the sauce.

Peel the pineapple, taking care to remove the brown 'eyes'. Cut into slices, about 1 cm (½ inch) thick, then remove the core. Sprinkle with pepper to taste.

Heat the remaining butter in a heavy-based frying pan and add the pineapple slices. Add the rest of the crème de cacao and set alight. When the flames have died down, add the sauce and heat through gently. Cut the pineapple slices into bite-sized pieces and allow to cool slightly.

Carefully unmould the toffee baskets and place on individual serving plates. Fill with the pineapple and ice cream.

VANILLA ICE CREAM

4 egg yolks
100 g (3½ oz) caster sugar
250 ml (8 fl oz) milk
250 ml (8 fl oz) double cream
½ vanilla pod
few drops of vanilla extract

Whisk the egg yolks and sugar together in a bowl. Heat the milk and cream together in a saucepan until hot, then gradually add to the egg and sugar mixture, whisking all the time.

Return to the pan and add the vanilla pod and vanilla extract. Cook, stirring constantly, until the custard thickens enough to lightly coat the back of the wooden spoon; do not allow to boil or it will curdle.

Pour into a bowl, set over a larger bowl of iced water to cool, stirring occasionally. Strain through a fine sieve.

Transfer to an ice-cream maker and churn until firm. Alternatively freeze in a shallow container, whisking 2 or 3 times during freezing to ensure a smooth-textured result.

THE NORTH WEST

GILLIAN HUMPHREY • JAMES DOERING • JUDI GEISLER

PANEL OF JUDGES

Stephen Bull • Carl Davis • Loyd Grossman

WINNER

GILLIAN HUMPHREY'S MENU

STARTER

Creamy Lemon Grass and Basil Soup with Seafood, served with Garlic Croûtons

"I thought the soup worked very well indeed. I liked the delicacy
of the lemon grass" **Stephen Bull**

MAIN COURSE

Fillet of Lamb with Tarragon Marsala Sauce

Spiced Pumpkin Purée

Buttered Leek Spaghetti

Steamed Green Vegetables

"I loved the sauce and everything about that main course I thought was really good,
including the pumpkin purée" **Stephen Bull**

DESSERT

Hot Caribbean Fruits with Butterscotch Sauce, served with Cinnamon Ice Cream

"Brioche caramelised in butter and sugar is just pure, pure heaven" **Stephen Bull**

Gillian Humphrey comes from Heaten Mersey in Stockport. Gillian
is a paediatric surgeon at "Jimmy's" where she conducts research
into various strains of cancer in children. To relax from her stressful
work, Gillian enjoys singing lessons. In quieter moments she settles
down to embossing, an interest developed in America, and very useful
for greetings cards. Gillian's baby son, Jonathan, however, takes up
much of her time at the moment.

CREAMY LEMON GRASS AND BASIL SOUP WITH SEAFOOD

24 large raw prawns
16 green-lipped mussels (thawed if frozen)
40 g (1½ oz) butter
75 g (3 oz) shallot, finely chopped
1 clove garlic, crushed
300 ml (½ pint) dry white wine
3 lemon grass stalks, bruised
1 kaffir lime leaf
15-30 ml (1-2 tbsp) lemon juice, to taste
300 ml (½ pint) single cream
30 ml (2 tbsp) shredded basil leaves
2 rashers sweet-cured back bacon, derinded
  and chopped
2 egg yolks
salt and freshly ground black pepper

Garlic Croûtes:
50 g (2 oz) butter
1 clove garlic, crushed
4-6 slices French bread
30 ml (2 tbsp) finely chopped basil

Shell and de-vein the prawns, reserving the shells.

To make the stock, melt 25 g (1 oz) of the butter in a saucepan, add the prawn shells and fry until pink. Add half of the chopped shallot with the garlic and cook until translucent. Add 300 ml (½ pint) water, the wine, lemon grass and kaffir lime leaf. Bring to the boil, reduce the heat and simmer for 30 minutes. Strain the stock and adjust the flavour with lemon juice.

Meanwhile prepare the garlic croûtes. Melt the butter in a pan, add the garlic and cook until softened. Add the bread slices and fry until golden on both sides; drain on kitchen paper. Toss in the chopped basil and keep warm. Bring the stock to the boil in a large pan. Add the prawns and cook until just pink, about 2-3 minutes. Remove with a slotted spoon and set aside. Add the mussels to the stock, heat through, then remove and set aside. Add the cream and shredded basil and simmer for 2-3 minutes. Meanwhile, cook the remaining shallot and the bacon in the rest of the butter until tender.

To serve, add the onion and bacon to the soup, with the prawns and mussels. Heat through, then transfer the seafood to warmed soup plates. Off the heat, work the egg yolks into the soup. Season with salt and pepper to taste and ladle over the seafood. Serve immediately, with the garlic croûtes.

FILLET OF LAMB WITH TARRAGON MARSALA SAUCE

2 lamb (loin) fillets, each about 225 g (8 oz)
15 g (½ oz) unsalted butter
20-30 rashers sweet-cured streaky bacon,
  derinded
1 packet spinach leaves, about 125 g (4 oz)
30-45 ml (2-3 tbsp) tarragon mustard

Sauce:
300 ml (½ pint) lamb stock
15 g (½ oz) chopped tarragon
150 ml (¼ pint) Marsala
15-30 ml (1-2 tbsp) redcurrant jelly
15 ml (1 tbsp) crème fraîche or mascarpone

To Garnish:
tarragon sprigs

Melt the butter in a frying pan, add the lamb fillets and brown evenly; remove and drain.

Stretch the bacon rashers with the back of a knife. Arrange them overlapping on a board to form 2 sheets (the same length as the lamb fillets). Blanch the spinach leaves in boiling water for 30 seconds, plunge into cold water to refresh, then drain thoroughly. Spread a thin layer of mustard over the bacon. Arrange the spinach leaves in a layer on top.

Place a lamb fillet at one end of each spinach and bacon 'sheet', then roll up. Wrap loosely in foil and set aside until required.

Place the lamb parcels in a roasting tin and cook in a preheated oven at 190°C (375°F) mark 5 for 20-25 minutes, according to taste.

Meanwhile, prepare the sauce. Put the stock in a pan with half of the chopped tarragon and boil to reduce by half. Add the Marsala and, again, reduce by half. Strain through a fine sieve into a clean pan, pressing the tarragon with the back of a wooden spoon to extract the juices.

Allow the cooked lamb to rest for 5 minutes before carving. Add the juices from the roasting tin to the sauce. Add the redcurrant jelly and heat, stirring, to dissolve. Whisk in the crème fraîche or mascarpone and reduce to the desired consistency. Stir in the remaining tarragon.

To serve, cut each lamb fillet into 6 slices. Arrange 3 slices on each warmed serving plate and surround with the sauce. Garnish with tarragon and serve with the accompaniments.

Note: Tarragon mustard is readily available, but you can prepare your own milder version if preferred. Mix 45 ml (3 tbsp) wholegrain mustard with 45 ml (3 tbsp) mild French mustard. Add 30 ml (2 tbsp) chopped fresh tarragon and 15 ml (1 tbsp) tarragon vinegar. Store in a jar in the refrigerator for up to 1 month.

SPICED PUMPKIN PURÉE

1 small butternut squash
salt and freshly ground black pepper
freshly grated nutmeg
15-30 ml (1-2 tbsp) mascarpone cheese

Peel and dice the squash. Place in an ovenproof dish, cover and bake in a preheated oven at 180°C (350°F) mark 4 for about 45 minutes, until soft.

Mash the squash, adding salt, pepper and nutmeg to taste. Beat in the mascarpone cheese to give a creamy texture. Serve piping hot.

Note: I prefer the flavour of butternut squash to that of English pumpkin. Baking enhances its sweet flavour, and doesn't result in a mushy texture.

BUTTERED LEEK SPAGHETTI

225 g (8 oz) leeks
½ red pepper, cored and seeded
15 g (½ oz) butter, melted
salt and freshly ground black pepper

Trim the leeks and cut into long thin strips, to resemble spaghetti. Cut the red pepper into 12 batons, each about 2.5 cm (1 inch) long. Steam the vegetables until tender.

To serve, toss the leeks in the melted butter. Season with salt and pepper to cook. Twirl the leeks into small mounds and arrange the red pepper batons on top. Serve at once.

Lime Sherbet in Pepper Tuile Baskets with Hot Cherries
ASHLEY WILSON'S DESSERT (Regional Heat)

*Duck Breast with Dried Cherry and Orange Sauce,
Potato Rosti and Thyme-scented Courgettes*

HOLLY SCHADE'S MAIN COURSE (Semi-Final)

Quails baked in Red Peppers with Little Corn Muffins
MARION MACFARLANE'S STARTER (Semi-Final)

Skewered Oysters and Scallops with a Sweet Pepper Sauce
MARION MACFARLANE'S STARTER (Final)

HOT CARIBBEAN FRUITS WITH BUTTERSCOTCH SAUCE

1 mango
½ paw-paw
1 navel orange
125-175 g (4-6 oz) pineapple
2 bananas
lemon juice, for sprinkling
50 g (2 oz) butter
4 slices brioche, each 1 cm (½ inch) thick
30-60 ml (2-4 tbsp) Malibu, to taste

Butterscotch Sauce:

40 g (1½ oz) soft brown sugar
75 g (3 oz) golden syrup
150 ml (¼ pint) single cream

To Serve:

Cinnamon Ice Cream (see right)
herb sprigs, to decorate

First make the sauce. Put the sugar, syrup and cream in a heavy-based pan over a low heat until the sugar is dissolved, then simmer for 3-4 minutes; set aside.

Meanwhile, peel, stone and dice the mango; peel, deseed and slice the paw-paw. Peel the orange, removing all white pith, then cut out the segments free from the membrane over a bowl to catch the juice. Peel, core and chop the pineapple into 2.5 cm (1 inch) pieces. Peel and slice the bananas and toss with the lemon juice to prevent discolouration.

Melt 25 g (1 oz) of the butter and toss the brioche slices in the melted butter. Bake in a preheated oven at 180°C (350°F) mark 4 for about 10 minutes until crisp and golden brown; watch carefully as the brioche slices will quickly brown (and burn if overdone).

Meanwhile, melt the remaining butter in a frying pan, add the mango, paw-paw, orange and pineapple; sauté for 1 minute. Add the banana and sauté for a further 1-2 minutes or until the fruit is beginning to soften. Stir in the reserved orange juice, butterscotch sauce and Malibu, to taste. Arrange the toasted brioche on warmed serving plates and drizzle over some of the sauce. Arrange the fruit around the brioche. Place a generous scoop of cinnamon ice cream on each brioche slice. Serve immediately, garnished with herb sprigs.

CINNAMON ICE CREAM

300 ml (½ pint) milk (preferably creamy
  Jersey or Guernsey)
1 cinnamon stick
5 ml (1 tsp) ground cinnamon
3 egg yolks
65 g (2½ oz) vanilla sugar
185 ml (6 fl oz) single cream

Put the milk in a heavy-based pan with the cinnamon stick and ground cinnamon. Bring to the boil, lower the heat and simmer gently for 30 minutes. Allow to cool, then strain.

Beat the egg yolks and sugar together in a bowl until thick and creamy. Add the cream to the strained milk and bring to the boil. Pour onto the egg yolk mixture, whisking constantly. Stand the bowl over a pan of simmering water and stir until the custard thickens, approximately 10 minutes. Cool, then freeze in an ice-cream maker.

Note: If you do not have an ice-cream maker, freeze in a suitable container, whisking periodically during freezing to break down the ice crystals and ensure an even-textured result.

The North West

Gillian Humphrey • James Doering • Judi Geisler

Panel of Judges

Stephen Bull • Carl Davis • Loyd Grossman

James Doering's Menu

Starter

*Cheese Choux Pastries filled with Wild Mushrooms in Madeira,
on a Frisée and Orange Salad*

"I thought the mushroom filling was excellent, I mean top class" **Stephen Bull**

Main Course

Rolled Fillets of Sole and Mixed Peppers on a Cream and Chive Sauce

Carrots with Parsley

Steamed Mangetouts

"The sole was perfect" **Stephen Bull**

Dessert

Individual Chocolate Pecan Pies, served with Maple Ice Cream

"The pudding was flawless" **Loyd**

James Doering from Southport is a former FutureCooks finalist. Sixteen-year-old James is a student at King George V College, where he is studying biology, sociology and French. An enthusiastic musician, James plays the clarinet in the music group at St Peter's Church. He has recently completed his Duke of Edinburgh Bronze Award which involved hiking thirty miles over two days and camping overnight.

CHEESE CHOUX PASTRIES FILLED WITH WILD MUSHROOMS IN MADEIRA

Choux Pastry:
65 g (2½ oz) strong plain flour
pinch of cayenne
150 ml (¼ pint) water
50 g (2 oz) butter, in pieces
2 eggs (size 1), beaten
65 g (2½ oz) Gruyère cheese, grated
beaten egg, to glaze

Filling:
15 g (½ oz) dried porcini mushrooms,
  chopped if large
40 g (1½ oz) butter
175 g (6 oz) onions, finely chopped
2 cloves garlic, crushed
175 g (6 oz) open cup mushrooms, chopped
175 g (6 oz) oyster mushrooms, chopped
2.5 ml (½ tsp) chopped thyme
salt and freshly ground black pepper
freshly grated nutmeg
150 ml (¼ pint) Madeira
90 ml (3 fl oz) double cream

To Serve:
1 small head frisée
2 oranges (preferably ruby-red)
30 ml (2 tbsp) extra-virgin olive oil

For the filling, put the dried mushrooms in a small bowl and pour on about 350 ml (12 fl oz) hot water to cover. Leave to soak for 30 minutes.

To make the sauce, melt the butter in a saucepan, add the onions and garlic and cook gently for about 5 minutes until softened and pale golden. Stir in all of the fresh mushrooms, then add the soaked mushrooms, together with their soaking water; there should be about 250 ml (8 fl oz). Add the thyme and season with salt, pepper and a generous grating of nutmeg. Pour in the Madeira and cover the pan with a tight-fitting lid. Let the mushrooms cook as slowly as possible

for 1½ hours; the liquid should barely simmer; check from time to time that it hasn't evaporated and add a little more water if necessary.

To make the choux pastry, sift the flour with the cayenne and a pinch of salt onto a piece of paper. Put the water and butter in a medium saucepan over a gentle heat until the butter has melted and the mixture comes to the boil. Turn the heat off and immediately tip in the flour, beating vigorously with a wooden spoon. Continue beating until the mixture forms a smooth ball. Beat in the eggs a little at a time, until you have a smooth, shiny paste. (It should have a dropping consistency – you may not need to add all of the egg.) Fold in 50 g (2 oz) of the cheese and season with salt, pepper and cayenne.

Place heaped spoonfuls of the choux pastry on a lightly greased baking sheet, spacing them well apart, to make 12 buns. Brush with a little beaten egg, then sprinkle with the rest of the cheese. Bake near the top of a preheated oven at 200°C (400°F) mark 6 for 10 minutes. Increase the temperature to 220°C (425°F) mark 7, and bake for a further 20 minutes.

Meanwhile, prepare the salad. Roughly tear the frisée into a bowl. Peel the oranges, removing all white pith, then slice crosswise into thin rounds. Add to the frisée. Season with salt and pepper and toss with the oil.

Split the choux pastries horizontally. Stir the cream into the mushroom filling, then use to fill the choux buns. Serve with the frisée and orange salad.

ROLLED FILLETS OF SOLE AND MIXED PEPPERS ON A CREAM AND CHIVE SAUCE

12 sole fillets, each about 50 g (2 oz),
*   skinned*
1 large lemon
½ red pepper
½ green pepper
½ yellow pepper

Sauce:
90 ml (3 fl oz) dry white wine
15 ml (1 tbsp) Noilly Prat
1 small shallot, finely chopped
250 ml (8 fl oz) fish stock
200 ml (7 fl oz) double cream
salt and freshly ground pepper
22 ml (1½ tbsp) finely chopped chives

To Garnish:
snipped chives

Place the sole fillets in a shallow dish. Grate 5 ml (1 tsp) zest from the lemon, then squeeze the juice and sprinkle the lemon juice and zest over the sole. Leave to marinate in a cool place for 2 hours.

Halve, core and deseed the peppers, then cut into thin strips. Blanch in boiling water for 3 minutes, then refresh under cold water.

To make the sauce, put the wine, Noilly Prat and shallot in a saucepan and simmer to reduce by half. Add the fish stock and reduce to one quarter. Stir in the cream and let the sauce simmer for 5 minutes until slightly thickened. Strain the sauce through a fine sieve or muslin and season with salt and pepper. Stir in the chopped chives.

Lay the sole fillets on a board and place 3 pepper strips, one of each different colour, on top. Roll up and place, seam-side down, in a steamer. Steam for 6-8 minutes.

To serve, ladle the chive sauce onto warmed serving plates and arrange the sole fillets on top. Serve immediately, garnished with chives.

CARROTS WITH PARSLEY

40 g (1½ oz) unsalted butter
2 shallots, finely chopped
4 large carrots, cut into 3 mm (⅛ inch) thick
*   slices*
½ clove garlic, crushed
salt and pepper
30 ml (2 tbsp) chopped parsley

Melt the butter in a pan, add the shallots and sweat for 2-3 minutes. Add the carrots and stir to coat in the butter. Add the garlic and 100 ml (3½ fl oz) water. Cover and cook gently for 15-20 minutes. Season with salt and pepper. Add the parsley and cook for a further 3 minutes. Serve at once.

INDIVIDUAL CHOCOLATE PECAN PIES

Pastry:
65 g (2½ oz) plain flour
pinch of salt
50 g (2 oz) butter
20 g (¾ oz) icing sugar
1 egg yolk (size 4)

Filling:
65 g (2½ oz) plain chocolate
25 g (1 oz) unsalted butter
2 eggs
120 ml (4 fl oz) maple syrup
few drops of vanilla essence
135 g (4½ oz) pecan nuts

To Serve:
Maple Ice Cream

For the pastry, put the flour and salt in a bowl and rub in the butter, then mix in the icing sugar. Work in the egg, adding a little water if necessary to yield a smooth, pliable, but not sticky dough. Wrap in cling film and leave to rest in the refrigerator for 20-30 minutes.

Roll out the pastry thinly on a lightly floured surface and use to line 4 loose-bottomed individual flan tins, 10 cm (4 inches) in diameter and 2.5 cm (1 inch) deep. Line the pastry cases with foil, fill with baking beans and bake blind in a preheated oven at 200°C (400°F) mark 6 for 10 minutes. Remove the beans and foil and bake for a further 6-7 minutes. Allow to cool. Reduce the oven temperature to 180°C (350°F) mark 4.

To make the filling, melt the chocolate with the butter in a small bowl over a pan of hot water. Meanwhile, whisk the eggs, maple syrup and vanilla essence together in a bowl. Stir in the melted chocolate mixture, then fold in the nuts.

Divide the filling between the pastry cases and bake for 30 minutes, until the filling is slightly puffed up in the centre and just set. Serve with the ice cream.

MAPLE ICE CREAM

3 egg yolks
90 ml (3 fl oz) maple syrup
300 ml (½ pint) whipping cream

Put the egg yolks into a bowl and whisk, using an electric beater, until pale and thick.

Meanwhile, heat the maple syrup in a small saucepan. Boil for 2-3 minutes until the syrup registers 110°C (225°F) on a sugar thermometer, ie when a drop of it will form a thread when pulled between the finger and thumb.

Remove the syrup from the heat and immediately pour onto the egg yolks, whisking constantly. Whisk for a further 2-3 minutes until the mixture is cool and very thick. Whip the cream until it holds its shape, then fold it into the maple mixture. Freeze in an ice-cream maker, according to the manufacturer's directions. Alternatively pour the mixture into a freezerproof container and freeze until firm. Remove from the freezer 5-10 minutes before serving to soften slightly.

THE NORTH WEST

GILLIAN HUMPHREY • JAMES DOERING • JUDI GEISLER

PANEL OF JUDGES

Stephen Bull • Carl Davis • Loyd Grossman

JUDI GEISLER'S MENU

STARTER

Mushroom Puffs with Red Pepper Sauce

"I did like the red pepper relish" **Stephen Bull**

MAIN COURSE

Turbot with a Herb Topping on a Beurre Blanc

Carrots with Fresh Ginger

Leeks in Vermouth

Buttered Noodles

"It worked very well because the fish was treated with such respect
and simplicity" **Stephen Bull**

DESSERT

St Clement's Mousse with Caramel Oranges

"A brilliant dessert" **Carl Davis**

Judi Geisler comes from Heaton Moor near Stockport. Judi trains senior management in financial and commercial skills, a role which involves her travelling throughout the country. In her spare time she often lends a hand with the family fishmongery business. Judi also enjoys time with her daughter Lucy – a visit to the Science Museum in nearby Manchester is always popular.

MUSHROOM PUFFS WITH RED PEPPER SAUCE

Choux Pastry:
65 g (2½ oz) strong plain flour
pinch of salt
50 g (2 oz) butter
150 ml (¼ pint) water
2 eggs, beaten (size 1)
25 g (1 oz) Gruyère cheese, grated

Filling:
25 g (1 oz) dried porcini mushrooms
225 g (8 oz) mixed mushrooms, roughly
  chopped
25 g (1 oz) butter
15 ml (1 tbsp) plain flour
90 ml (3 fl oz) dry sherry
salt and freshly ground black pepper
freshly grated nutmeg

Sauce:
2 red peppers
15 ml (1 tbsp) olive oil
125 g (4 oz) shallots, finely chopped
30 ml (2 tbsp) crème fraîche

To Garnish:
watercress sprigs

For the filling, soak the dried porcini in 250 ml (8 fl oz) warm water for 30 minutes.

To make the choux pastry, sift the flour and salt onto a piece of paper. Put the water and butter into a medium pan and heat gently until melted. Bring to the boil, take the pan off the heat and immediately add the flour all at once, beating constantly until the mixture forms a smooth ball.

Beat in the eggs, a little at a time, until the mixture forms a glossy paste. (It should have a dropping consistency – you may not need to add all of the egg.) Stir in the grated cheese and season with a little salt and pepper.

Grease a baking tray, then sprinkle with water; the steam created will help the puffs to rise. Put 12 heaped spoonfuls of the choux paste onto the baking tray, spacing well apart to allow for expansion. Bake in a preheated oven at 200°C (400°F) mark 6 for about 35 minutes until rich brown in colour and quite firm. Cut a slit in the side of each puff to allow the steam to escape. Cool on a wire rack.

Meanwhile make the mushroom filling. Drain the porcini, reserving the liquid and chop roughly. Melt the butter in a large frying pan and fry all of the mushrooms for 2-3 minutes. Sprinkle in the flour and cook, stirring, for a further 2 minutes. Stir in the sherry and enough of the reserved soaking liquid to make a thick mushroom sauce. Season with salt, pepper and freshly grated nutmeg. Cook gently until the mushrooms are tender.

To make the red pepper sauce, grill the peppers under a preheated hot grill until the skins are blackened. Place in a tightly covered bowl and leave to cool, then peel away the skins and chop the flesh into small pieces. Heat the olive oil in a pan, add the shallots and fry gently for 5 minutes. Add the chopped peppers and fry for a further 10 minutes until the shallots and peppers are very soft. Stir in the crème fraîche and season with salt and pepper to taste. If a smooth sauce is required, whizz in a blender or food processor until smooth.

To assemble, put the puffs into a hot oven for 1 minute, to heat through. Warm the mushroom filling and the red pepper sauce in separate pans. Spoon a small amount of red pepper sauce onto each plate. Top with 3 puffs and fill each puff with mushrooms. Garnish with watercress sprigs.

TURBOT WITH A HERB TOPPING ON A BEURRE BLANC

4 turbot steaks, each 150-175 g (5-6 oz)
30 ml (2 tbsp) chopped parsley
15 ml (1 tbsp) chopped dill
15 ml (1 tbsp) chopped thyme
5 ml (1 tsp) finely chopped rosemary leaves
600 ml (1 pint) fish stock

Sauce:
60 ml (4 tbsp) reduced fish stock
15 ml (1 tbsp) white wine vinegar
1 shallot, chopped
225 g (8 oz) unsalted butter, chilled and cut into small pieces
salt and freshly ground black pepper
juice of ½ lemon, or to taste

Mix the chopped herbs together and press 15 ml (1 tbsp) onto the top of each turbot steak. Bring the fish stock to the boil in a steamer.

To make the sauce, put the stock, vinegar and shallot in a wide pan and bring to the boil, then boil to reduce to about 30 ml (2 tbsp). Strain and return to the pan. Place over a low heat and whisk in the butter, a piece at a time, until the sauce is thick and creamy. Season with salt and pepper to taste and add enough lemon juice to sharpen the sauce. Transfer to a bowl set over a pan of hot, but not boiling, water to keep warm for no longer than 15 minutes, whisking gently from time to time.

Meanwhile, steam the turbot over the fish stock for 8-10 minutes, depending on thickness. The fish should be just opaque in the middle. Remove the skin from the fish and take out the central bone, taking care to avoid disturbing the topping too much.

To serve, spread some of the sauce on each warmed serving plate and place the fish on top. Serve at once, with the accompaniments.

CARROTS WITH FRESH GINGER

350 g (12 oz) carrots, cut into matchsticks
salt and freshly ground black pepper
15 g (½ oz) butter
15 g (½ oz) fresh root ginger, peeled and finely chopped
15 ml (1 tbsp) sugar

Cook the carrots in boiling salted water for 5-10 minutes until just tender. Drain, then plunge into a bowl of cold water to refresh. Drain and return to the pan with the butter, ginger and sugar. Stir over a low heat until the carrots are well coated. Cover and simmer for 2 minutes, then check the seasoning and serve.

LEEKS IN VERMOUTH

350 g (12 oz) leeks, thinly sliced
25 g (1 oz) butter
60 ml (2 fl oz) dry vermouth

Melt the butter with the vermouth in a saucepan. Add the leeks and cook, stirring, for 2-3 minutes until the leeks are tender and the liquid has evaporated. Serve at once.

BUTTERED NOODLES

225 g (8 oz) thin egg noodles
15 g (½ oz) butter
freshly ground black pepper

Bring a large pan of salted water to the boil. Add the noodles, cover and take off the heat. Leave the noodles to stand and cook in the residual heat for 6 minutes, then drain and stir in the butter. Sprinkle with pepper and serve immediately.

ST CLEMENT'S MOUSSE WITH CARAMEL ORANGES

Mousse:
1 sachet powdered gelatine
finely grated rind of 1 lemon (see note)
juice of 2 lemons
juice and finely grated rind of 1 orange
3 eggs, separated
125 g (4 oz) caster sugar
250 ml (8 fl oz) double cream, lightly whipped

Caramel Oranges:
2 large oranges
200 g (7 oz) sugar
30 ml (2 tbsp) Grand Marnier

Candied Peel:
finely pared rind of 1 lemon
finely pared rind of 2 oranges
15 ml (1 tbsp) sugar

To make the mousse, sprinkle the gelatine over the lemon and orange juices in a small bowl and leave to soften. In a large bowl, whisk the egg yolks, sugar and grated lemon and orange rinds together until thick and pale. Stand the gelatine bowl in a pan of hot water until the gelatine dissolves, then strain onto the egg yolks. Stir until the mixture starts to set, then fold in the whipped cream. Whisk the egg whites until stiff but not dry, then fold into the mousse. Divide the mixture between 4 individual moulds and leave in the refrigerator for at least 1 hour to set.

To prepare the caramel oranges, finely pare the rind from the oranges; reserve for the candied peel. Peel all the pith from the oranges, then cut crosswise into thin slices; halve each slice. Put the sugar in a heavy-based pan with 120 ml (4 fl oz) water and dissolve over a low heat, then slowly bring to the boil. (Remove any sugar crystals from the sides of the

pan with a dampened pastry brush.) Boil until the syrup caramelises to a rich brown colour. Take the pan off the heat.

Meanwhile, mix the Grand Marnier with 90 ml (3 fl oz) cold water. As soon as the syrup caramelises, take off the heat and add the diluted Grand Marnier, protecting your hand with a cloth because it will splutter furiously. Reheat, stirring constantly until the caramel dissolves, then remove from the heat and dip the base of the pan into cold water to stop further cooking. Once the caramel is cool, pour it over the orange slices and chill in the refrigerator for at least 1 hour.

To prepare the candied peel, cut the reserved lemon and orange rind into julienne strips. Blanch in boiling water for 2 minutes, then drain. Dissolve the sugar in 30 ml (2 tbsp) water in a small heavy-based pan over a low heat. Bring to the boil and add the citrus rind strips. Leave to simmer until all of the water has evaporated. Transfer the candied peel to a large plate and leave to cool.

To serve, dip the moulds into hot water for a few seconds, then turn out onto 4 large serving plates. Surround with the caramel orange slices and decorate with candied peel strips.

Note: Pare the rind from the other lemon for the mousse and set aside for the candied peel.

SEMI-FINAL

HOLLY SCHADE • DAVID HICKIN • GILL TUNKLE

PANEL OF JUDGES

Willi Elsener • Jill Dando • Loyd Grossman

WINNER

HOLLY SCHADE'S MENU

STARTER

Squid Ink Risotto with Monkfish and Prawns

"...a stunning dish... it was just really out of this world" **Willi Elsener**

MAIN COURSE

Duck Breast with Dried Cherry and Orange Sauce

Potato Rösti

Thyme-scented Courgettes

"The duck breasts were perfectly cooked... a very, very nice dish" **Willi Elsener**

DESSERT

Lemon Tart with Crème Fraîche Ice Cream

"...lovely, refreshing" **Jill Dando**

SQUID INK RISOTTO WITH MONKFISH AND PRAWNS

Use the special Italian risotto rice – Arborio – for this starter. It readily absorbs plenty of liquid, resulting in a wonderful creamy texture.

30 ml (2 tbsp) olive oil
1 small onion, finely chopped
2 cloves garlic, finely chopped
225 g (8 oz) fennel, cored and finely chopped
225 g (8 oz) Arborio rice
750 ml (1¼ pints) fish stock
2 sachets of squid ink
225 g (8 oz) monkfish fillet, skinned and cubed
125 g (4 oz) Parmesan cheese, freshly grated
freshly ground black pepper
25 g (1 oz) butter
12 large prawns, or 4 medium langoustines

To Garnish:
parsley or chives

Heat the olive oil in a heavy-based pan, add the onion and sweat until softened. Add the garlic and fennel and cook, stirring occasionally, for 3 minutes. Add the rice and cook, stirring constantly, for 2 minutes.

Meanwhile, heat the stock in another saucepan. Add about 250 ml (8 fl oz) of the hot stock to the rice and cook, stirring, until absorbed. Add the squid ink and monkfish. Continue adding the stock a ladleful at a time, as each addition is absorbed. Continue until the rice is plump and tender yet still has some bite. (You may not need to add all of the stock.) Stir in the Parmesan, pepper and butter.

Meanwhile cook the prawns or langoustines in a large pan of boiling water for 4 minutes, or until pink.

To serve, divide the risotto between individual serving bowls and garnish with the prawns or langoustines and parsley or chives.

DUCK BREAST WITH DRIED CHERRY AND ORANGE SAUCE

3-4 duck breasts
salt and freshly ground black pepper
45 ml (3 tbsp) cherry preserve

Sauce:
350 ml (12 fl oz) duck or brown stock
350 ml (12 fl oz) red wine
125 ml (4 fl oz) port
2.5 ml (½ tsp) thyme leaves
30 ml (2 tbsp) grated orange rind
juice of ½ orange
75 g (3 oz) dried cherries
10 ml (2 tsp) arrowroot

To make the sauce, boil the stock to reduce by half; then add the rest of the ingredients except the cherries and arrowroot. Simmer until reduced by half, then add the cherries and cook for a further 10 minutes. Mix the arrowroot with 5 ml (1 tsp) water, then add to the sauce and stir over a medium heat until thickened. Keep warm until ready to serve.

Rub the fat side of the duck breasts with salt and pepper, then spread with the cherry preserve. Preheat a heavy-based frying pan, then add the duck breasts, skin-side down, and sear over a high heat for 2 minutes. Turn the duck breasts over and sear the other side for 2 minutes. Transfer to a roasting tin and cover lightly with foil.

Cook the duck in a preheated oven at 200°C (400°F) mark 6 for 10-15 minutes until cooked through but still pink in the centre. Slice the duck breasts and fan out on warmed individual serving plates. Pour on the sauce and serve at once, with the potato rösti, and courgettes flavoured with thyme.

POTATO RÖSTI

4 large potatoes
1 medium sweet potato (orange-fleshed)
1 onion, finely chopped
salt and freshly ground black pepper
15 ml (1 tbsp) lemon juice
50 g (2 oz) butter, melted
15 ml (1 tbsp) clarified butter, for cooking

Peel all of the potatoes, cut into quarters and cook in boiling water for 5 minutes. Drain and rinse in cold water to stop further cooking. Allow to cool for 15 minutes.

Grate the cooled potatoes and place in a bowl with the onion, seasoning, lemon juice and melted butter. Mix thoroughly.

Heat the clarified butter in a heavy-based frying pan. Place heaped spoonfuls of the potato mixture in the pan and shape into rounds, about 7.5 cm (3 inches) in diameter. Cook over a moderate heat for about 5 minutes, pressing down firmly with a spatula to hold their shape. Turn the rösti over and cook the other side until golden brown and crisp. Drain on kitchen paper and serve at once.

LEMON TART

Pastry:
125 g (4 oz) plain flour
pinch of salt
grated rind of 1 lemon
25 g (1 oz) icing sugar
75 g (3 oz) butter, in pieces
1 egg yolk, mixed with 15 ml (1 tbsp)
*   iced water*

Filling:
6 eggs (size 2)
225 g (8 oz) caster sugar
125 g (4 oz) unsalted butter, in pieces
grated rind of 3 lemons
150 ml (¼ pint) freshly squeezed lemon juice

To make the pastry, put the flour, salt, lemon rind, icing sugar and butter in a food processor and process, using the pulse button, just until the mixture resembles coarse breadcrumbs. With the motor running, add the egg yolk and water, processing briefly until the mixture just holds together, but does not quite form a ball. Pull the dough together with your hands and quickly form a ball.

Flatten the dough then roll out between 2 sheets of cling film and use to line a 23 cm (9 inch) loose-bottomed flan tin. Trim the edges and prick the base with a fork. Chill in the refrigerator for 30 minutes.

Line the pastry case with greaseproof paper and fill with baking beans or rice. Bake in a preheated oven at 200°C (400°F) mark 6 for 10 minutes. Remove the paper and beans, then return the pastry case to the oven for a further 10 minutes, to dry and cook the base. Cool on a wire rack. Lower the oven temperature to 190°C (375°F) mark 5.

To make the filling, place all the ingredients in a bowl over a pan of simmering water. Whisk until well blended and continue stirring until the mixture thickens slightly – just enough to coat the back of a wooden spoon. Stand the flan tin on a baking sheet. Pour the filling into the pastry case and bake in the oven for 25 minutes, or until set. Allow to cool slightly.

Serve warm or cold, cut into wedges, with the ice cream.

CRÈME FRAÎCHE ICE CREAM

225 g (8 oz) crème fraîche
125 ml (4 fl oz) milk
45 ml (3 tbsp) lemon juice
150 g (5 oz) caster sugar

Put all of the ingredients in a food processor and process briefly until evenly blended and smooth. Transfer to a bowl and chill until cold, then freeze in an ice-cream maker according to the manufacturer's instructions. Serve in scoops, with the lemon tart.

Note: If you do not have an ice-cream maker freeze in a shallow container, whisking 2-3 times during freezing to break down the ice crystals and ensure an even-textured result.

THE FIRST
SEMI-FINAL
HOLLY SCHADE • DAVID HICKIN • GILL TUNKLE

PANEL OF JUDGES
Willi Elsener • Jill Dando • Loyd Grossman

DAVID HICKIN'S MENU

STARTER
*Brandad with Poached Quail's Eggs, Salad
and a Coriander Vinaigrette*

"The brandad was extremely well done, and the combination
was lovely" **Jill Dando**

MAIN COURSE
Osso Bucco with Creamy Saffron Rice and Gremolata

"A nice combination. The rice was great" **Jill Dando**

DESSERT
Amaretti Ice Cream with Chocolate Sauce

"The ice cream was sensational" **Willi Elsener**

BRANDAD WITH POACHED QUAIL'S EGGS

Brandad:

225 g (8 oz) salt cod fillet
1 small potato, peeled and chopped
60-75 ml (4-5 tbsp) olive oil
1 clove garlic, crushed
30-45 ml (2-3 tbsp) milk
freshly ground white pepper

To Serve:

selection of salad and herb leaves, (eg lamb's
  lettuce, endive, coriander)
45 ml (3 tbsp) olive oil
15 ml (1 tbsp) wine vinegar
2.5 ml (½ tsp) wholegrain mustard
4 quail's eggs
a little oil and butter, for frying
croûtons (see note)
15 ml (1 tbsp) freshly pared Parmesan
  cheese flakes

Soak the salt cod in cold water to cover overnight.

The next day, drain the fish and pat dry with kitchen paper. Drain. Flake the fish, discarding any skin and bone. Cook the potato in boiling water until tender, then drain and mash until smooth; set aside.

Heat 30 ml (2 tbsp) olive oil in a heavy-based saucepan. Add the cod and garlic and heat gently, stirring constantly, for about 5-10 minutes until the fish is quite dry. Add the remaining oil and milk alternately in small quantities, beating constantly until absorbed. Cook, stirring, for 3-5 minutes, adding the mashed potato in small amounts and mixing thoroughly to form a smooth, light paste. (It may not be necessary to add all of the potato.) Season with pepper to taste.

In the meantime, prepare the salad leaves and arrange on individual serving plates. Shake the oil, vinegar and mustard together in a screw-topped jar to make a dressing.

Heat the oil and butter in a small frying pan and lightly fry the quail's eggs for about 1 minute. Place the quail's eggs on the salad leaves and scatter over the croûtons and Parmesan cheese shreds. Drizzle the dressing around the edge of the plate. Shape the brandad into quenelles, using 2 tablespoons. Position on the serving plates and serve immediately.

Note: To prepare the croûtons, fry small cubes of bread in oil flavoured with a little crushed garlic until crisp and golden. Drain on kitchen paper.

OSSO BUCCO WITH CREAMY SAFFRON RICE AND GREMOLATA

4 pieces of shin of veal
25 g (1 oz) plain flour, for coating
30 ml (2 tbsp) oil
6 tomatoes
450 ml (¾ pint) veal stock (approximately)

Saffron Rice:
125 g (4 oz) Arborio rice
pinch of saffron threads
45 ml (3 tbsp) warm veal stock
salt and freshly ground black pepper
50 ml (2 fl oz) double cream
25 g (1 oz) butter
40 g (1½ oz) freshly grated Parmesan cheese

Gremolata:
5 ml (1 tsp) chopped anchovy fillets (about 2 fillets)
5 ml (1 tsp) chopped capers
15 ml (1 tbsp) grated lemon rind, blanched for 1 minute
1 clove garlic, crushed
20 ml (4 tsp) chopped parsley

Toss the veal in the flour until well coated on all sides. Heat the oil in a heavy-based frying pan, add the veal and seal quickly over a high heat until well browned on all sides. Transfer to a casserole dish. Immerse the tomatoes in boiling water for 30 seconds, then remove and peel away the skins. Cut into quarters, remove the seeds, then add to the veal. Pour in sufficient stock to just cover the meat. Cover and cook in a preheated oven at 170°C (325°F) mark 3 for 1½-2 hours, until tender.

Meanwhile, for the rice, soak the saffron in the warm stock for about 20 minutes.

Mix together the ingredients for the gremolata, place in a bowl and set aside.

Put the rice into a saucepan with the saffron and soaking liquid, salt, pepper and 300 ml (½ pint) water. Bring to the boil and simmer, covered, for about 20 minutes until the rice is tender and the liquid is absorbed. Check from time to time that it isn't dry and add a little more water if necessary. Stir in the cream, butter and Parmesan.

Arrange the meat and tomatoes on warmed serving plates and top with the gremolata. Shape the rice into quenelles, using 2 tablespoons, and position on the plates. Serve at once.

AMARETTI ICE CREAM WITH CHOCOLATE SAUCE

Ice Cream:
300 ml (½ pint) double cream
125 g (4 oz) caster sugar
30 ml (2 tbsp) Amaretto di Saronno liqueur

Base:
50 g (2 oz) amaretti biscuits
15-30 ml (1-2 tbsp) shelled pistachio nuts

Sugar Cage:
225 g (8 oz) sugar (preferably lump sugar)
7.5 ml (1½ tsp) liquid glucose

Chocolate Sauce:
150 ml (¼ pint) double cream
1 vanilla pod
150 ml (¼ pint) milk
225 g (8 oz) plain chocolate, in pieces

To Decorate:
few raspberries

Place all of the ingredients for the ice cream in an ice-cream maker and churn for 20-30 minutes until firm. Alternatively, place in a bowl and beat thoroughly until smooth, then freeze in a suitable container, beating two or three times during freezing to break down the ice crystals and ensure an even-textured result.

For the base, crush the amaretti biscuits and pistachio nuts together between two sheets of greaseproof paper, using a rolling pin; set aside.

For the caramel cages, dissolve the sugar in 30 ml (2 tbsp) water in a heavy-based pan over a low heat, then bring to the boil. Add the liquid glucose and cook until the syrup turns a pale caramel colour, ie until it registers 165°C (330°F) on a sugar thermometer. Take off the heat and leave to rest for 2 minutes.

Meanwhile with your hand, spread the tiniest amount of oil over the back of a ladle. Dip a spoon into the caramel, let the excess run off then trickle the thread to and fro over the ladle to create a basket. Repeat this procedure if necessary, then allow to cool and gently twist the cage free. Repeat to make a further 3 cages and place into an airtight container. Do not leave them in a humid atmosphere, otherwise they will go sticky and collapse.

To make the sauce, warm the milk in a saucepan, add the vanilla pod, remove from the heat and leave to infuse for about 15 minutes. Discard the vanilla pod and stir in the cream. Add the chocolate and heat, stirring, until melted and smooth.

To serve, place a 7.5 cm (3 inch) biscuit cutter on an individual serving plate and spoon in a quarter of the crushed biscuit mixture. Spread evenly with the back of a spoon to form a base, then remove the ring. Repeat to make 4 bases. Place one or two scoops of ice cream on each base and surround with the chocolate sauce. Decorate with the caramel cages and raspberries. Serve at once.

SEMI-FINAL

HOLLY SCHADE • DAVID HICKIN • GILL TUNKLE

PANEL OF JUDGES

Willi Elsener • Jill Dando • Loyd Grossman

GILL TUNKLE'S MENU

STARTER

*Chicken Mousse with Mango
and a Lemon Ginger Sabayon*

"Sensational" **Willi Elsener**

MAIN COURSE

*Pan-fried Fillet of Tuna,
served with a Basil Salsa*

Potato Galette

Confit of Fennel and Olives

"I think it's an outstanding dish" **Willi Elsener**

DESSERT

*Peppered Pineapple, flambéed in Kirsch,
served with a Pineapple Sorbet crowned with Angel's Hair*

"The sorbet combined with the pineapple... it was very, very good" **Willi Elsener**

CHICKEN MOUSSE WITH MANGO AND A LEMON GINGER SABAYON

Mousse:
2 chicken breasts, about 450 g (1 lb) total
weight, filleted and skinned
salt and freshly ground white pepper
2 egg whites, beaten
120 ml (4 fl oz) double cream, chilled
120 ml (4 fl oz) milk
2.5 cm (1 inch) cube of fresh root ginger,
peeled and grated (see note)
1-2 mangoes, peeled and thinly sliced

Lemon Ginger Sayabon:
2 egg yolks
125 g (4 oz) butter, clarified and melted
juice of ½ lemon
120 ml (4 fl oz) double cream
30 ml (2 tbsp) chicken stock
salt and freshly ground black pepper

To Garnish:
few chives

Put the chicken in a food processor, add salt and pepper, and process until smooth. Mix in the egg whites, cream, milk and ginger. Pass through a drum or tamis sieve, or a food mill; this is important and will result in a light-textured mousse when cooked.

Line 4 ramekins with a layer of mango slices and spoon in the chicken mousse. Stand the ramekins in a bain-marie or roasting tin containing enough boiling water to come two thirds of the way up the sides of the dishes. Cover the tin loosely with foil and cook in a preheated oven at 180°C (350°F) mark 4 for about 30 minutes until firm to the touch. Remove from the bain-marie to stop the cooking process.

Meanwhile make the lemon ginger sauce. Whisk the egg yolks with 45 ml (3 tbsp) water in a saucepan over a gentle heat until thickened and doubled in volume. Remove from the heat and slowly add the melted butter, whisking constantly. Continue whisking over the heat and add the lemon juice, cream and chicken stock. Season with salt and pepper to taste. Whisk until the sauce resembles a custard in consistency.

To serve, gently unmould each mousse into the centre of a large warmed serving plate and surround with the sauce. Place a couple of chives on each mousse and position 2 or 3 slices of mango to one side on the sauce. Serve immediately.

Note: To ensure a fibre-free pulp, use a fine grater to grate the ginger.

PAN-FRIED FILLET OF TUNA, SERVED WITH A BASIL SALSA

For this recipe, use tuna fillets cut from the middle to the tapering end of the fillet if possible.

4 tuna fillets, each about 175 g (6 oz)

Marinade:
60 ml (4 tbsp) extra-virgin olive oil
juice of 1 lemon
handful of fresh mixed herbs (bay, thyme,
 oregano, parsley, chervil)
2 cloves garlic, very roughly chopped
salt and freshly ground black pepper

Basil Salsa:
90 ml (3 fl oz) agrumato (see note)
25 ml (1 fl oz) lemon juice
5 ml (1 tsp) coriander seeds, crushed
8 basil leaves, shredded
2 tomatoes, skinned, seeded and diced

To Finish:
a little oil for cooking

Wipe the tuna fillets with kitchen paper, then place in a shallow dish. Mix together the ingredients for the marinade, then pour over the tuna to cover evenly. Cover the dish with cling film and leave to marinate for at least 2 hours.

To prepare the basil salsa, heat the oil gently in a small pan. Add the lemon juice. Remove from the heat, add the crushed coriander seeds and leave to infuse. Set aside the shredded basil and diced tomato.

To cook the tuna, heat a little oil in a heavy-based frying pan or griddle until searing hot. Lift the tuna out of the marinade, discarding any bits of herb that may be sticking to the fillets. Add the tuna to the pan, pressing down firmly to sear the fillets. Cook for 1 minute each side only; the tuna should still be pink in the centre.

To serve, place a warm potato galette in the centre of each large warmed serving plate and position a tuna fillet on top. Add the basil and tomato to the basil salsa and spoon over the tuna and sparingly around the plate. Arrange the confit of fennel and olives on the plate and serve at once.

Note: Agrumato is extra-virgin olive oil flavoured with pressed lemons. If unobtainable, use a good quality extra-virgin olive oil instead.

POTATO GALETTES

4 medium potatoes
1 clove garlic, finely chopped
1 shallot, finely chopped
salt and freshly ground black pepper
25 g (1 oz) butter
150 ml (¼ pint) fish stock

Grease a 12 inch (30 cm) oval gratin dish. Peel the potatoes and cut into wafer-thin slices; do not rinse them, as the starch in the potato helps the gratin stick together.

Shape 4 potato galettes in the gratin dish. Start by overlapping 5 potato slices in a circle to form a base to each galette. Sprinkle with half of the garlic, shallot and salt and pepper, then make another slightly smaller potato layer on top. Sprinkle over the remaining garlic and shallot and dot with a few small knobs of butter. Carefully pour in the fish stock which should just cover the base of the gratin dish.

Cook uncovered in a preheated oven at 160°C (325°F) mark 3 for about 50 minutes until the galettes are golden brown and crisp, and slightly charred at the edges. Serve at once.

CONFIT OF FENNEL AND OLIVES

For this accompaniment, use the young thin fennel shoots if available, rather than the rounded bulbs.

4 young thin fennel bulbs
salt and freshly ground black pepper
25 ml (1 fl oz) olive oil
8 black olives, halved and stoned (see note)

Trim the young fennel bulbs and leave whole; if using bulbous fennel, trim, core and cut into 5 mm (¼ inch) slices. Blanch in boiling salted water for 3 minutes, then quickly refresh in a bowl of cold water. Drain, pat dry and place in a clean pan with the olive oil. Gently heat through, then add the olives. Season with pepper to taste.

Note: For optimum flavour, use olives which have been preserved in wild fennel flavoured olive oil; use the oil in the recipe too.

PEPPERED PINEAPPLE FLAMBÉED IN KIRSCH, SERVED WITH A PINEAPPLE SORBET

Pineapple Sorbet:

1 large or 2 medium pineapples, enough for
  675 g (1½ lb) peeled and cored weight
275 ml (9 fl oz) stock syrup (see right)
juice of ½ lemon

Pineapple Flambé:

1 medium pineapple
freshly ground black pepper
25 g (1 oz) unsalted butter
50 ml (2 fl oz) kirsch

To Decorate:

16 angelica diamonds
Spun Sugar (optional – see right)

To make the sorbet, top and tail the pineapple, then peel away the skin, removing the brown 'eyes'. Quarter, core and cut up into chunks. Put in a food processor with the stock syrup and lemon juice. Process until smooth and creamy, then pass through a nylon sieve into a bowl. Transfer to an ice-cream machine and churn according to the manufacturer's instructions for about 25 minutes until firm.

Transfer to a plastic freezerproof container, cover and place in the freezer until ready to serve. If you do not have an ice-cream maker, freeze the sorbet in a suitable container, whisking several times during freezing to break down the ice crystals and ensure an even-textured result.

For the pineapple flambé, put 4 large serving plates in the freezer to chill. Top and tail the pineapple, then peel away the skin, making sure you remove the brown 'eyes'. Cut into slices, about 1 cm (½ inch) thick. Cut out the central core from each slice, then sprinkle with a little black pepper. Heat the butter in a frying pan and, when hot, add the pineapple slices to heat through and colour slightly. Pour over the kirsch and immediately set alight. Once the flames have died down, the dish can be assembled.

To serve, place a pineapple slice in the centre of each large chilled serving plate and spoon a little of the pan juices into the central hollow. Place 4 scoops or quenelles of sorbet around the plate. Position angelica diamonds in between. For an elegant presentation, top the pineapple slices with spun sugar to resemble angel's hair.

Stock Syrup: Put 100 g (3½ oz) granulated sugar and 250 ml (8 fl oz) water in a heavy-based saucepan and dissolve over a low heat. Bring to the boil and boil steadily for 2 minutes. Cool and use as required.

Spun Sugar: Dissolve 250 g (9 oz) caster sugar in 90 ml (6 tbsp) water in a heavy-based pan over a low heat, then bring to the boil. Add 50 ml (2 fl oz) liquid glucose and cook the syrup to a pale caramel; ie until it registers 165°C (330°F) on a sugar thermometer. Take off the heat and leave to rest for 2 minutes. Hold 2 forks back to back, dip into the syrup, then quickly trickle the threads to and fro over a sheet of non-stick baking parchment to form spun sugar, or angel's hair. Use within 1 hour or keep in an airtight container with a drying agent. Do not leave in a humid atmosphere.

THE SECOND
──── SEMI-FINAL ────
CLARE ASKAROFF • GILLIAN HUMPHREY • DEREK MORRIS

PANEL OF JUDGES

Stewart Cameron • Sue MacGregor • Loyd Grossman

WINNER

CLARE ASKAROFF'S MENU

STARTER

*Gingered Crab Cakes, with Sweet Pepper Sauce
and Roasted Pepper Salad*

"The crab cakes were particularly good, they were
nice and crunchy" **Stewart Cameron**

MAIN COURSE

*Best End of Lamb with Roasted Beetroot and Garlic,
served with a Beetroot Jus*

Celeriac with Coriander

Saffron Tagliatelle with Poppy Seeds

"The main course was absolutely superb" **Sue MacGregor**

DESSERT

Apple Streusel Pies with Pecan and Maple Ice Cream

"The streusel pudding was just a revelation... that ice cream,
it was dreamy" **Sue MacGregor**

GINGERED CRAB CAKES WITH SWEET PEPPER SAUCE

125 g (4 oz) waxy potato (eg Romano)
225 g (8 oz) very fresh crab meat (mixed white and brown meat)
30 ml (2 tbsp) chopped parsley
5 ml (1 tsp) grated fresh root ginger
2.5 ml (½ tsp) freshly ground nutmeg
pinch of cayenne
salt and freshly ground black pepper
30-45 ml (2-3 tbsp) seasoned flour
groundnut oil for shallow-frying

Sweet Pepper Sauce:
15 ml (1 tbsp) olive oil
2 cloves garlic, crushed
1 shallot, finely chopped
2 medium red peppers, seeded and chopped
¼ large red chilli, finely chopped (optional)
4-5 basil leaves
salt and freshly ground black pepper
300 ml (½ pint) light fish stock
60 ml (2 fl oz) double cream

To Serve:
flat-leaved parsley or basil leaves
Roasted Pepper Salad (see right)

Cook the potato in boiling water for 10 minutes. Drain and allow to cool a little, then grate coarsely and place in a bowl. Add the crab meat, parsley, ginger, nutmeg, cayenne and seasoning; mix together using a fork, taking care not to damage the potatoes or crab meat.

Carefully shape into 8 flat cakes, squashing the mixture together with your hands. Dip the crab cakes in seasoned flour to coat. Place on a tray and chill in the refrigerator for at least 10 minutes, or until ready to cook.

To make the sweet pepper sauce, heat the olive oil in a pan, add the garlic and shallot and sweat until softened. Add the red peppers, chilli if using, basil, seasoning and stock. Bring to the boil, lower the

heat and simmer for 20 minutes. Transfer to a food processor or blender and process until smooth. Pass through a sieve into a small pan and add the cream. Set aside. Reheat gently before serving.

To cook the crab cakes, heat the groundnut oil in a heavy-based frying pan. Add the crab cakes and fry for about 2-3 minutes each side until crisp and golden brown. Drain on kitchen paper. Garnish with parsley or basil and serve with the red pepper sauce and roasted pepper salad.

Note: The chilli gives the sauce a slight kick, but you can omit it if preferred.

ROASTED PEPPER SALAD

1 red pepper
1 yellow pepper
1 orange pepper
extra-virgin olive oil
salt and freshly ground black pepper

Halve the peppers and remove the seeds. Place cut-side down in a roasting tin and drizzle with olive oil. Place under a preheated hot grill for about 10 minutes until the skins are blackened and blistered. Immediately place in a bowl, cover tightly and leave to stand for about 15 minutes; the steam created will help to lift the skins.

Peel the peppers and finely shred the flesh. Place in a bowl with 15 ml (1 tbsp) olive oil, season liberally with salt and pepper, and toss to mix. Leave until ready to serve; do not refrigerate.

BEST END OF LAMB WITH ROASTED BEETROOT AND GARLIC

For this recipe, you need well trimmed French-style best ends of lamb, with their bones scraped clean.

2 best ends of neck of lamb
350-450 g (¾-1 lb) extra lamb bones,
  chopped up
salt and freshly ground black pepper
3-4 rosemary sprigs
15 g (½ oz) butter, softened
3-4 thyme sprigs, leaves only

Beetroot Jus:
1 raw beetroot, cut into small pieces
12 black peppercorns
6 cloves
2 bay leaves
5 ml (1 tsp) wine vinegar
5 ml (1 tsp) caster sugar

Roasted Beetroot and Garlic:
4-6 raw baby beetroots (unpeeled but
  washed)
60 ml (4 tbsp) extra-virgin olive oil
150 ml (¼ pint) milk
8 garlic cloves, unpeeled
8 shallots, peeled
4 thyme sprigs
30 ml (2 tbsp) caster sugar
15 ml (1 tbsp) sherry vinegar

To Finish Sauce:
50 g (2 oz) cold unsalted butter, diced

First make the beetroot jus. Place all the ingredients in a pan with 300 ml (½ pint) cold water and bring to the boil. Lower the heat and simmer for 20 minutes. Cool, then strain. If necessary, make up to 150 ml (¼ pint) with cold water. Set aside until required for the sauce.

Season the lamb bones liberally, then place in a roasting tin with the rosemary sprigs. Roast in the oven at 200°C (400°F)

mark 6 for 30-45 minutes.

Meanwhile, rub the meat all over with the softened butter. Season liberally with salt and pepper and press the thyme leaves into the meat. Leave to stand for a while.

Cut the beetroot into quarters, place in a roasting tin and drizzle with 30 ml (2 tbsp) olive oil. Roast in the oven for 10 minutes. Meanwhile bring the milk to the boil, add the garlic and cook for 1 minute. Drain and skin the garlic cloves. Add to the roasting tin containing the beetroot. Add the shallots, thyme and remaining 30 ml (2 tbsp) olive oil. Season generously with salt and pepper, baste well and return to the oven for 20 minutes.

Stand the meat on top of the lamb bones and roast in the oven for 10-15 minutes. Transfer the meat to a warmed dish, cover with foil and leave to rest in a warm place.

Sprinkle the roasted vegetables with the sugar and sherry vinegar. Place on the hob and allow to sizzle for about 1 minute to caramelise. Transfer to a warmed serving dish with a slotted spoon. Keep warm. Deglaze the roasting tin with half of the beetroot jus.

Remove the lamb bones from their roasting tin and deglaze the tin with the remaining beetroot jus. Strain the liquids from both roasting tins into a saucepan. Boil to reduce a little, then whisk in the butter a little at a time until the sauce is glossy and a little thicker. Adjust the seasoning.

Carve the meat into thick slices and arrange on warmed serving plates. Surround with the caramelised vegetables. Pour on the sauce and serve with the accompaniments.

Celeriac with Coriander

1 celeriac root, about 675 g (1½ lb)
juice of 1 lemon
salt and freshly ground black pepper
25-50 g (1-2 oz) butter
30 ml (2 tbsp) soured cream
10 ml (2 tsp) coarse-grain mustard
1 spring onion, finely chopped
30-45 ml (2-3 tbsp) chopped coriander leaves

Peel the celeriac and cut into chunks. Quickly immerse in a bowl of cold water with the lemon juice added to prevent discolouration.

Cook the celeriac in boiling salted water for 10-15 minutes until tender; drain well. Roughly mash the celeriac with the butter. Add all the rest of the ingredients and season liberally. Stir well and serve piping hot.

Saffron Tagliatelle with Poppy Seeds

100 g (3½ oz) plain white flour
1.25 ml (¼ tsp) salt
1 egg (size 2)
1 sachet powdered saffron

To Serve:
15 ml (1 tbsp) extra-virgin olive oil
5 ml (1 tsp) poppy seeds

Place the flour, salt, egg and saffron in a food processor. Whizz for 1-2 minutes until a smooth, soft dough is formed. Turn onto a floured board and knead for about 1 minute. Place the dough in a floured polythene bag and leave to rest for at least 30 minutes.

Divide the dough into 3 pieces; keep each wrapped until required. Pass each piece through a pasta machine, gradually narrowing the setting from 1 to 6. Then pass through the tagliatelle cutters. Hang to dry.

Cook the pasta in plenty of boiling salted water for 1-2 minutes until *al dente*; tender but firm to the bite. Drain well. Return the pasta to the pan, drizzle with olive oil and add the poppy seeds. Toss to mix, then serve.

APPLE STREUSEL PIES

Pastry:
125 g (4 oz) plain flour
50 g (2 oz) unsalted butter
10 ml (2 tsp) icing sugar
1 egg yolk
15 ml (3 tsp) cold water (approximately)

Filling:
50 g (2 oz) plain flour
25 g (1 oz) unsalted butter
50 g (2 oz) caster sugar
225 g (8 oz) cooking apples
15 g (½ oz) sultanas
150 ml (¼ pint) double cream

Topping:
15 g (½ oz) caster sugar
2.5 ml (½ tsp) ground cinnamon

To Finish:
icing sugar, for dusting

Grease four 10 cm (4 inch) loose-bottomed fluted flan tins.

To make the pastry, sift the flour into a bowl and rub in the butter until the mixture resembles fine breadcrumbs. Stir in the icing sugar. Add the egg yolk and sufficient cold water to mix to a soft dough. Wrap in cling film and chill in the refrigerator for 10-15 minutes.

Meanwhile, make the crumble for the filling. Sift the flour into a bowl and rub in the butter until it resembles fine bread-crumbs. Stir in the caster sugar.

Peel, core and thinly slice the apples. Roll out the pastry thinly and use to line the individual flan tins. Sprinkle 10 ml (2 tsp) crumble mixture over the base of each pastry case. Divide the apples and sultanas between the pastry cases, arranging them neatly in layers. Pour on the cream. Sprinkle the remaining crumble mixture evenly over the fruit. (You may not need to use all of it.)

For the topping, mix the sugar and cinnamon together and sprinkle on top of the flans.

Place the flan tins on a baking sheet and bake in the centre of a preheated oven at 200°C (400°F) mark 6 for 20 minutes. Lower the setting to 190°C (375°F) mark 5 and cook for a further 10 minutes. Leave to stand for a few minutes, then carefully remove from the tins and place on serving plates dusted with icing sugar. Accompany with the ice cream.

PECAN AND MAPLE ICE CREAM

50 g (2 oz) pecan nuts
2 eggs, separated
30 ml (2 tbsp) caster sugar
150 ml (¼ pint) Jersey or double cream
30 ml (2 tbsp) maple syrup

Toast the pecan nuts under the grill, then chop (not too finely). Set aside a few chopped nuts for decoration.

In a large bowl, whisk the egg whites until very stiff. Whisk in the sugar 15 ml (1 tbsp) at a time. In another bowl, lightly whip the cream.

Add the cream, egg yolks, maple syrup and chopped nuts to the egg white mixture and carefully fold in.

Transfer the mixture to an ice-cream maker and churn for 15-20 minutes. Turn into a freezerproof container and place in the freezer until required. Unless serving within 2 hours, transfer the ice cream to the refrigerator 30 minutes before serving to soften slightly. Serve sprinkled with the reserved chopped nuts.

THE SECOND
SEMI-FINAL
CLARE ASKAROFF • GILLIAN HUMPHREY • DEREK MORRIS

PANEL OF JUDGES
Stewart Cameron • Sue MacGregor • Loyd Grossman

GILLIAN HUMPHREY'S MENU

STARTER
Sweet and Sour Tomato Soup
"It was light and had a wonderful flavour, sweet and sour,
and slightly crunchy" **Sue MacGregor**

MAIN COURSE
Pan-fried Barbary Duck Breast with Madeira Sauce
Puréed Potato and Apple
Caramelised Shallots
Lemon-glazed Carrots and Courgettes
"The duck was wonderfully cooked" **Sue MacGregor**

DESSERT
Bruléed Lime Curd Cream Tartlets with Raspberry Coulis
"...it tasted absolutely wonderful" **Sue MacGregor**

SWEET AND SOUR TOMATO SOUP

4 large beefsteak tomatoes
15 ml (1 tbsp) olive oil
2 cloves garlic, chopped
425 g (15 oz) can chopped tomatoes, sieved
15 ml (1 tbsp) sugar
30-45 ml (2-3 tbsp) balsamic vinegar
45 ml (3 tbsp) chopped basil
salt and freshly ground black pepper
30 ml (2 tbsp) basil oil

Cut a thin slice off the top of each tomato and scoop out the flesh, leaving a 5 mm (¼ inch) thick shell. Deseed and finely chop the tomato flesh.

Heat the olive oil in a pan and sauté the garlic until softened. Add the chopped tomato flesh, together with the sieved canned tomatoes. Bring to the boil, lower the heat and simmer gently for about 3 minutes. Add the sugar and balsamic vinegar to taste. Simmer for 1-2 minutes, stirring to dissolve the sugar. Add the chopped basil and simmer for 5-10 minutes. Season with salt and pepper to taste.

Meanwhile, stand the tomato shells in a baking tin and trickle the basil oil over them. Bake in a preheated oven at 190°C (375°F) mark 5 for 5 minutes to heat through.

To serve, stand each tomato shell on a warmed serving plate and fill with the tomato soup. Garnish with basil leaves and serve at once, with crusty bread if desired.

PAN-FRIED BARBARY DUCK BREAST WITH MADEIRA SAUCE

4 boned Barbary duck breasts, each about
   175 g (6 oz)
5 ml (1 tsp) ground star anise
5 ml (1 tsp) ground Szechuan pepper
salt
15 g (½ oz) unsalted butter

Sauce:
300 ml (½ pint) duck or poultry stock
150 ml (¼ pint) Madeira
30 ml (2 tbsp) rowan jelly

Score the skin of the duck breasts and rub with the spices and salt; set aside.

For the sauce, simmer the stock in a saucepan until reduced by half. Add the Madeira and, again, reduce by half.

Meanwhile, melt the butter in a heavy-based frying pan. Place the duck breasts in the pan, skin-side down, and cook for about 5 minutes until sealed and browned. Turn over and cook for 2-3 minutes until browned. Transfer to a roasting tin and cook in a preheated oven at 190°C (375°F) mark 5 for 10-20 minutes, according to taste and the size of the fillets. Leave to rest for 5 minutes before carving.

Skim off the fat from the meat juices in the tin, then add them to the sauce. Strain the sauce into a clean pan and add the rowan jelly. Heat, stirring, until melted.

To serve, slice each duck breast lengthwise and fan out on warmed serving plates. Pour on the sauce and serve with the accompaniments.

PURÉED POTATO AND APPLE

450 g (1 lb) potatoes, peeled
1 small Bramley apple
10 ml (2 tsp) sugar, or to taste
25 g (1 oz) butter
30-45 ml (2-3 tbsp) single cream
salt and freshly ground black pepper

Cook the potatoes in boiling salted water for 15-20 minutes until soft. Drain and return to the pan to dry out a little.

Meanwhile, peel, core and slice the apple. Place in a heavy-based pan with the sugar and 30 ml (2 tbsp) water. Cook gently until soft and pulpy.

Mash the potatoes with the butter and cream. Stir in the apple and season with salt and pepper to taste. Serve piping hot.

CARAMELISED SHALLOTS

10-20 shallots (unpeeled)
20 g (¾ oz) butter
4 large pinches of caster sugar
salt and freshly ground black pepper

Add the shallots to a pan of boiling water and cook for 2-3 minutes. Drain and leave until cool enough to handle, then remove the skins.

Place the shallots, butter and sugar in a heavy-based pan. Cover with a tight-fitting lid and cook over a low heat for about 10 minutes until tender and caramelised, shaking the pan from time to time to prevent sticking.

LEMON-GLAZED CARROTS AND COURGETTES

225 g (8 oz) carrots, peeled and cut into batons
225 g (8 oz) courgettes, trimmed and chopped
salt and freshly ground black pepper
15 g (½ oz) butter
10 ml (2 tsp) sugar
juice of ½ lemon

Add the carrots to a pan of boiling salted water and cook for 5-6 minutes. Add the courgettes and cook for 2-3 minutes. Drain thoroughly and return to the pan. Add the butter, sugar and lemon juice. Toss over a moderate heat for 2-3 minutes to glaze. Check the seasoning and serve at once.

BRULÉED LIME CURD CREAM TARTLETS WITH RASPBERRY COULIS

This pastry is rich and a little difficult to roll out, so handle it as little as possible. The quantities below make twice as much pastry as you need; freeze the other half for another occasion.

Pastry:
250 g (9 oz) plain flour
pinch of salt
25 g (1 oz) ground almonds
15 ml (1 tbsp) icing sugar
150 g (5 oz) chilled unsalted butter, diced
1 egg yolk

Filling:
3 eggs (size 1), plus 3 egg yolks
scant 75 g (3 oz) vanilla caster sugar
finely grated rind and juice of 3 limes
15 g (½ oz) butter
185 ml (6 fl oz) double cream
225 g (8 oz) raspberries

Raspberry Coulis:
225 g (8 oz) raspberries
50 g (2 oz) sugar
squeeze of lemon juice (optional)

To Decorate:
icing sugar, for dusting
8 mint leaves
30 ml (2 tbsp) single cream

Mix the flour, salt, ground almonds and icing sugar together in a bowl. Rub in the butter until the mixture resembles breadcrumbs. Add the egg yolk and about 30 ml (2 tbsp) cold water, to form a smooth dough. Wrap in cling film and place in the freezer for 20-30 minutes to chill thoroughly until firm enough to handle.

Roll out the pastry thinly and use to line 4 individual loose-bottomed flan tins. Line with greaseproof paper and baking beans and bake blind in a preheated oven at 200°C (400°F) mark 6 for 10 minutes. Remove the paper and beans and return to the oven for 5 minutes or until the bases are cooked. Leave to cool in the tins, then turn out.

Meanwhile, make the filling. Whisk the eggs, extra yolks and sugar together in a bowl until thick and creamy. Add the lime rind and juice, and stand the bowl over a pan of simmering water for about 10 minutes, whisking occasionally. When the lime curd has thickened just enough for the whisk to leave a trail when lifted, remove the bowl from the heat. Stir in the butter and allow to cool.

For the raspberry coulis, put the raspberries in a shallow dish, sprinkle with the sugar and leave to macerate for about 1 hour. Press through a nylon sieve into a bowl to remove the pips. Add a squeeze of lemon juice to taste.

To finish the tartlets, whip the cream until thick and fold into the lime curd. Fill the tartlet cases with raspberries, reserving 4 for decoration. Cover with the lime curd and chill in the refrigerator for 30 minutes, if time.

Dust the tartlets with icing sugar. Protect the edges of the pastry with foil and place under a preheated high grill to caramelise the sugar; this will take about 10 seconds. Allow to cool.

Place each tartlet on a large serving plate and decorate with the reserved raspberries and mint leaves. Surround with the raspberry coulis, dot with the cream and feather with a skewer. Serve at once.

SEMI-FINAL

CLARE ASKAROFF • GILLIAN HUMPHREY • DEREK MORRIS

PANEL OF JUDGES
Stewart Cameron • Sue MacGregor • Loyd Grossman

DEREK MORRIS' MENU

STARTER

*Tiger Prawns with White Cabbage,
Coconut and Shrimp Paste*

"...an unusual combination... I thought it worked very well indeed,
and it looked good too" **Sue MacGregor**

MAIN COURSE

Sliced Fillet of Venison with Damson Sauce

Steamed Herb Rolls

*Steamed Carrot and Swede
with Szechuan Pepper*

"...excellent, excellent sauce" **Sue MacGregor**

DESSERT

*Robin Pears with White Wine, Saffron and Cream,
served with Polenta Biscuits*

"The pudding worked extremely well. The biscuits were
a revelation" **Sue MacGregor**

TIGER PRAWNS WITH WHITE CABBAGE, COCONUT AND SHRIMP PASTE

16-20 raw tiger prawns, according to size
75 ml (5 tbsp) sunflower oil
1 large shallot, finely chopped
1 clove garlic, finely chopped
5-10 ml (1-2 tsp) shrimp paste
5-10 ml (1-2 tsp) laos
350 g (12 oz) white cabbage, cored and
 shredded
250 ml (8 fl oz) coconut milk
sea salt and freshly ground black pepper

To Garnish:
2 spring onions, shredded
cayenne or paprika, for sprinkling

Remove the heads from the prawns. Heat 15 ml (1 tbsp) of the oil in a pan, add the shallot and garlic and cook over a low heat for 2 minutes without browning. Add the shrimp paste and laos and cook for a further 1 minute. Bring to the boil, then add the cabbage. Cover and cook for 10 minutes. Remove the lid and allow most of the liquid to evaporate, stirring to prevent sticking. Adjust the seasoning and keep warm.

Heat the remaining 60 ml (4 tbsp) sunflower oil in a sauté pan until smoking. Add the prawns and stir-fry for about 3 minutes until bright pink. Drain on kitchen paper.

Make shallow mounds of cabbage on 4 warmed serving plates. Arrange the prawns on the cabbage and scatter the spring onion over the plate. Sprinkle lightly with cayenne or paprika. Serve at once.

SLICED FILLET OF VENISON WITH DAMSON SAUCE

450 g (1 lb) boned loin of venison
150 ml (¼ pint) good red wine
5-10 ml (1-2 tsp) juniper berries, lightly
 crushed
2.5 ml (½ tsp) sea salt
freshly ground black pepper
15 ml (1 tbsp) sunflower oil

Damson Sauce:
25 g (1 oz) damson cheese (or damson jam),
 cut into small pieces
10 ml (2 tsp) crème fraîche

To Garnish:
flat-leaved parsley

Cut the venison into 4 equal slices. Place in a shallow dish and pour over the red wine. Add the juniper berries, salt and a generous grinding of pepper. Stir, then cover and leave to marinate for 2 hours.

Remove the meat from the marinade and pat dry with kitchen paper; strain the marinade through a fine sieve and set aside. Heat the oil in a sauté pan over a high heat until smoking. Add the meat and cook quickly, turning constantly, for 4 minutes. Remove the meat from the pan and keep warm.

Add the marinade to the pan with the damson cheese. Simmer gently until the cheese has melted. Adjust the seasoning, remove from the heat and stir in the crème fraîche.

To serve, place the venison slices on warmed serving plates and pour on the damson sauce. Garnish with parsley and serve with the accompaniments.

STEAMED HERB ROLLS

150 g (5 oz) strong plain white flour
2.5 ml (½ tsp) sea salt
5 ml (1 tsp) sugar
7 g (¼ oz) fresh yeast
22 ml (1½ tbsp) sunflower oil
60-75 ml (4-5 tbsp) chopped mixed herbs (of your choice)
sunflower oil, for brushing

Place the flour and salt in a warmed mixing bowl. Put 50 ml (2 fl oz) tepid water in a small jug and add the sugar and yeast. Mix until smooth, then leave for about 10 minutes until frothy.

Make a well in the centre of the flour, and add the yeast mixture, oil and herbs. Mix until smooth, then knead thoroughly for 5 minutes. Cover the bowl with cling film and leave to rise in a warm place until doubled in volume, about 1 hour.

Turn onto a floured surface and roll out to a rectangle about 15 x 23 cm (6 x 9 inches). Brush the surface with a little sunflower oil, then roll up from a short side, like a Swiss roll. Cut across the roll into 4 equal pieces. Press a chopstick along the middle of each roll, parallel to the cut edges, almost to the work surface.

Line the base of the first tier of a two-tier steamer with foil, leaving a gap around the edge. Brush with oil and place the 4 rolls on the foil, leaving 2.5 cm (1 inch) between them. Leave to rise for 20 minutes, then place the covered steamer over boiling water and steam for 7 minutes.

STEAMED CARROT AND SWEDE WITH SZECHUAN PEPPER

225 g (8 oz) swede, peeled
225 g (8 oz) carrots, peeled
2.5 ml (½ tsp) sea salt
2.5 ml (½ tsp) Szechuan pepper, coarsely ground
15 g (½ oz) butter

Cut the swede and carrots into 5 mm (¼ inch) thick slices, then into 5 mm (¼ inch) wide strips. Place in a shallow dish that will fit inside the second tier of a two-tier steamer. Sprinkle with the salt and pepper. Steam (with the herb rolls) for 17 minutes. Transfer to a warm dish and dot with the butter.

ROBIN PEARS WITH WHITE WINE, SAFFRON AND CREAM

Robin pears are an indigenous East Anglian variety. If unobtainable, use another variety.

350 g (12 oz) bottled pears, preferably Robin
75 ml (5 tbsp) pear juice (from the bottled pears)
75 ml (5 tbsp) medium dry white wine
7.5 ml (1½ tsp) vanilla sugar
large pinch of saffron strands
30 ml (2 tbsp) double cream

To Decorate:
mint sprigs

Put the pear juice and wine in a saucepan and boil vigorously until reduced by half. Add the vanilla sugar.

Put the saffron strands into a mortar and add a little of the hot liquid. Leave to soak for a few minutes, then pulverize with the pestle. Add to the saucepan with the pear halves and heat through for 2 minutes. Just before serving, stir in the cream.

Arrange the pears on individual serving plates and pour over the sauce. Decorate with mint leaves and serve with the polenta biscuits.

Note: To make your own vanilla sugar, simply store a vanilla pod in a jar of caster sugar to impart flavour.

POLENTA BISCUITS

60 g (2¼ oz) polenta (maize flour)
35 g (1¼ oz) best plain flour
good pinch of baking powder
70 g (2¾ oz) icing sugar
pinch of salt
50 g (1¾ oz) unsalted butter, in pieces
5 ml (1 tsp) vanilla essence
1 (size 2) egg yolk

Put all of the dry ingredients into a mixing bowl. Rub in the butter, using the fingertips. Add the vanilla essence and egg yolk and mix to a stiff paste. Wrap in cling film and refrigerate for 30 minutes.

Roll out the dough on a floured surface to a 3 mm (⅛ inch) thickness; the dough may be a little difficult to handle as it is quite soft and sticky. Using a 4 cm (1½ inch) square biscuit cutter, cut out small biscuits. Transfer to a greased and floured baking sheet, leaving 2.5 cm (1 inch) between each biscuit to allow for spreading. Bake in a preheated oven at 180°C (350°F) mark 4 for 6 minutes or until golden. Immediately lift off the baking sheet and place on a wire rack to cool. Serve with the pears.

SEMI-FINAL

MARION MACFARLANE • GARETH RICHARDS • ASHLEY WILSON

PANEL OF JUDGES
Sonia Stevenson • Ken Livingstone • Loyd Grossman

WINNER

MARION MACFARLANE'S MENU

STARTER
Quails Baked in Red Peppers
Little Corn Muffins with Sun-dried Tomatoes
"The corn muffins were wonderful" **Loyd**

MAIN COURSE
Crispy Skin Salmon with Morels and Trompette de Mort
on a bed of Curly Kale with Spicy Puy Lentils
"I think that salmon is most probably the best salmon I've ever tasted...
it was absolutely magnificent" **Ken Livingstone**

DESSERT
Hazelnut Torte with Mascarpone and Bramble Coulis
"I thought that meringue was just heaven...
it was so beautiful and perfect" **Loyd**

"I thought it was a brilliant menu – all the flavours came
up to the colours" **Sonia Stevenson**

QUAILS BAKED IN RED PEPPERS

This is my interpretation of a dish I first ate many years ago on holiday in France. It is one of those rustic dishes that are deservedly becoming fashionable again. I try to buy free-range quail if possible. Many specialist outlets are now selling boned quail which are ideal. If small quail are unobtainable, use 2 large ones, halved, instead.

4 small boned quail
a little basil oil, or extra-virgin olive oil, for
  marinating
30 ml (2 tbsp) pine nuts
salt and freshly ground black pepper
a little ground coriander
freshly ground nutmeg
handful of basil leaves
2 large cloves garlic
4 small red peppers
60 ml (4 tbsp) extra-virgin olive oil (Italian)

To Serve:
herbs (chives, chervil, basil), to garnish
Corn Muffins (see right)

Rub the quail all over with basil oil and leave to marinate for a few hours, or overnight if possible.

Toast the pine nuts in a small frying pan over a moderate heat until lightly browned. Season the birds well with salt and pepper, a sprinkling of ground coriander and freshly ground nutmeg. Place 2-3 basil leaves and 6 pine nuts in each quail cavity. Crush one of the garlic cloves and divide between the 4 birds.

To prepare the peppers, cut off the tops, making an opening large enough to accept the quails; reserve the tops. Remove the core and seeds. Drizzle a little olive oil in each pepper and carefully place the quails inside. Cut the remaining garlic clove into 4 slices and add a sliver to each pepper. Replace the tops and stand the peppers in a shallow ovenproof dish. Drizzle the remaining olive oil over the peppers and cook in a preheated oven at 200°C (400°F) mark 6 for about 30-40 minutes, basting the peppers occasionally.

To serve, carefully lift the peppers on to warm serving plates, spoon over some of the juices and garnish with herbs and the remaining toasted pine nuts. Serve with the corn muffins to soak up all the delicious juices.

Note: As an alternative, halve, core and deseed 2 large red peppers and cook the quails in the pepper halves.

LITTLE CORN MUFFINS WITH SUN-DRIED TOMATOES

60 g (2¼ oz) cornmeal (coarse-ground)
65 g (2½ oz) plain flour
5 ml (1 tsp) sugar
7.5 ml (1½ tsp) baking powder
1.25 ml (¼ tsp) salt
1 small egg (size 5)
120 ml (4 fl oz) milk
15 ml (1 tbsp) corn oil
25 g (1 oz) sun-dried tomatoes in oil,
  drained

Stir all the dry ingredients together in a bowl and make a well in the centre. Beat the egg with the milk and oil, add to the well and mix into the flour to yield a smooth batter. Dry the excess oil from the tomatoes using kitchen paper, then chop finely and stir into the batter.

Spoon the batter into oiled small or medium muffin tins to half-fill the tins. Bake in a preheated oven at 220°C (425°F) mark 7 for 10-12 minutes until golden brown. Leave in the tins for a few minutes, then carefully remove and serve warm.

CRISPY SKIN SALMON WITH MORELS AND TROMPETTE DE MORT ON A BED OF CURLY KALE WITH SPICED PUY LENTILS

This way of cooking salmon gives a crispy skin which is delicious to eat.

575 g (1¼ lb) middle-cut salmon fillet, with skin
7.5 ml (1½ tsp) hazelnut oil
sea salt

Lentils:
125 g (4 oz) Puy lentils
25 g (1 oz) butter
50 g (2 oz) leek (white part only), shredded
1 clove garlic
2.5 ml (½ tsp) fennel seeds, freshly ground
2.5 ml (½ tsp) coriander seeds, freshly ground
2.5 ml (½ tsp) cardamom seeds, freshly ground
2.5 ml (½ tsp) cumin seeds, freshly ground
150 ml (¼ pint) chicken stock

Sauce:
12 small dried morels
12 dried trompette de mort
120 ml (4 fl oz) Noilly Pratt
150 ml (¼ pint) chicken stock
120 ml (4 fl oz) double cream
15 g (½ oz) butter

Kale:
5 ml (1 tsp) oil
25 g (1 oz) derinded bacon, finely chopped
125 g (4 oz) curly kale, finely chopped
4 juniper berries, crushed

Soak the lentils in cold water to cover for 2 hours. Cut the salmon fillet into four rectangular pieces and keep covered in a cool place until required.

To make the sauce, soak the dried mushrooms in warm water to cover for 30 minutes; drain. Simmer the Noilly Pratt in a pan until reduced by about two thirds. Add the stock and reduce again by about half. Add the cream and butter and bring to a simmer. Stir in the reconstituted mushrooms and cook gently until softened. Set aside to allow the flavours to infuse, until required.

To cook the lentils, melt the butter in a pan, add the leek and sauté until softened. Add the garlic and spices and cook for a further 1 minute. Drain the lentils and put into a saucepan with the stock and the leek and spice mixture. Cook for about 10 minutes until *al dente*, tender but firm to the bite.

To cook the curly kale, heat the oil in a wok, add the bacon and toss over a medium-high heat for 1 minute. Add the kale and juniper berries and toss over a moderate heat for 2-3 minutes until just wilted.

Meanwhile heat the hazelnut oil in a heavy-based frying pan until very hot. Place the salmon fillets, skin-side down, in the pan and cook for 1 minute then, using tongs, seal each of the other surfaces. Now place skin-side down for 2 minutes, turn and cook the opposite side for 1 minute, then turn again and cook skin-side down for a further 1-2 minutes; the skin should be dark brown and crisp.

To serve, place a mound of kale on each serving plate and position a portion of salmon on top. Place a spoonful of the lentils to one side and spoon the sauce and mushrooms around. Sprinkle the salmon with sea salt and serve at once.

HAZELNUT TORTE WITH MASCARPONE AND BRAMBLE COULIS

Torte:
2 egg whites (size 3)
1.25 ml (¼ tsp) baking powder
125 g (4 oz) caster sugar
125 g (4 oz) hazelnuts, coarsely ground

Filling:
250 g (9 oz) mascarpone cheese
10 ml (2 tsp) icing sugar
22 ml (1½ tbsp) blackberry liqueur

Bramble Coulis:
175 g (6 oz) blackberries
40 g (1½ oz) icing sugar
7.5 ml (1½ tsp) lemon juice
7.5 ml (1½ tsp) blackberry liqueur

To Decorate:
50 g (2 oz) bitter chocolate, melted
few whole blackberries
mint sprigs
chocolate rose leaves (optional – see right)

To make the torte, whisk the egg whites in a bowl until stiff. Whisk in the baking powder and half of the sugar, then carefully fold in the ground nuts and the rest of the sugar. Spoon onto baking sheets, lined with greaseproof paper or non-stick baking parchment, making two circles about 15 cm (6 inches) in diameter. Bake in a preheated oven at 180°C (350°F) mark 4 for about 30 minutes. Remove from the oven and allow to cool on the paper.

To make the bramble coulis, put the blackberries in a blender or food processor with the icing sugar and lemon juice and work to a purée. Pass through a sieve into a bowl to remove the pips, then add the liqueur and keep cool until required.

For the torte filling, mix the mascarpone with the icing sugar and liqueur. Invert one torte layer onto a serving plate and carefully spread with the filling. Place the other layer on top. Pipe fine lines of melted chocolate on top to decorate. To serve, cut the torte into wedges and place on individual serving plates. Surround with the blackberry coulis and decorate with chocolate leaves if using, blackberries and mint sprigs.

Note: Kirsch or crème de cassis can be used in place of the blackberry liqueur, but you may need to adjust the quantities according to taste.

Chocolate Rose Leaves: Using a paintbrush, paint the undersides of clean, dry rose leaves with melted chocolate. Leave in a cool place until set, then carefully peel the leaves away from the chocolate.

SEMI-FINAL

MARION MACFARLANE • GARETH RICHARDS • ASHLEY WILSON

PANEL OF JUDGES

Sonia Stevenson • Ken Livingstone • Loyd Grossman

GARETH RICHARDS' MENU

STARTER

*Medley of Fish Mousse
with a Champagne Butter Sauce*

MAIN COURSE

Grilled Breast of Duck with "Harvest Sauce"

Glazed Onions

Pecan Crêpes filled with Stir-fried Vegetables

"The crêpes were just fabulous" **Loyd**

DESSERT

*Lemon Shortcake filled with Lemon Cream,
served with a Lime Coulis*

"Wonderful pudding" Loyd

MEDLEY OF FISH MOUSSE WITH A CHAMPAGNE BUTTER SAUCE

15 g (½ oz) butter
225 g (8 oz) leeks (white part only), trimmed
  and chopped
225 g (8 oz) filleted white fish (eg sole or
  cod), cubed
1 egg white (size 2)
300 ml (½ pint) whipping cream
salt and freshly ground black pepper
½ cucumber, thinly sliced

Sauce:
300 ml (½ pint) Champagne
45 ml (3 tbsp) olive oil
125 g (4 oz) butter
10 ml (2 tsp) chopped dill
15 ml (1 tbsp) chopped chives

To Garnish:
1 tomato
4 cooked King prawns
dill sprigs

Line the bases of 4 ramekin dishes with buttered greaseproof paper discs. Melt the butter in a pan, add the leeks and cook gently for about 5 minutes until soft. Leave to cool.

Place the fish and egg white in a food processor and process until smooth. Pass through a sieve into a bowl.

Whip the cream until soft peaks form. Fold into the mousse with the leeks and season with salt and pepper to taste.

Divide the mixture between the ramekin dishes and top with overlapping cucumber slices. Cover with buttered greaseproof paper. Stand the ramekins in a steamer and cook for 10 minutes, or until set.

Meanwhile make the sauce. Put the Champagne, oil and butter in a saucepan and boil steadily until reduced by half. Add the chopped dill and chives.

For the tomato concassé garnish, immerse the tomato in boiling water for 30 seconds, then remove and peel away the skin. Halve, deseed and dice the flesh.

Unmould the mousses onto individual serving plates and surround with a circle of cucumber slices and the Champagne butter sauce. Garnish with the prawns, tomato concassé and dill. Serve at once.

GRILLED BREAST OF DUCK WITH "HARVEST SAUCE"

4 boneless duck breasts, each about 175 g
  (6 oz)
salt and freshly ground black pepper
15 ml (1 tbsp) finely chopped herbs (eg sage,
  thyme, parsley)
20 shallots (unpeeled)
25 g (1 oz) butter

Sauce:
600 ml (1 pint) duck or poultry stock
60 ml (4 tbsp) blackberry liqueur

To Garnish:
few blackberries

For the sauce, simmer the stock to reduce by about half.

To prepare the duck breasts, season with salt and pepper and press the finely chopped herbs evenly on to the flesh. Cook under a preheated high grill for about 4 minutes on each side until browned and crisp on the outside, but still pink in the middle.

Meanwhile, blanch the shallots in boiling water for 2-3 minutes, then drain and peel when cool enough to handle. Melt the butter in a pan, add the shallots and cook, shaking the pan frequently, for about 5 minutes until glazed.

Transfer the duck breasts to a warmed dish, cover and leave to rest in a warm place for 5-8 minutes, before carving.

Meanwhile, skim off excess fat from the grill pan and deglaze with the blackberry liqueur, stirring to scrape up the sediment. Add the juices to the reduced stock and reduce further if necessary, to the desired consistency.

To serve, slice the duck breasts diagonally and arrange on warmed serving plates. Pour on the sauce and garnish with the glazed onions and blackberries. Serve accompanied by the crêpes.

PECAN CREPES FILLED WITH STIR-FRIED VEGETABLES

Crêpes:
25 g (1 oz) plain flour
pinch of salt
2 eggs, beaten
300 ml (½ pint) milk
50 g (2 oz) pecan nuts, finely chopped

Vegetable Filling:
30 ml (2 tbsp) oil
1 clove garlic, crushed
2.5 cm (1 inch) piece fresh root ginger,
  grated
1 carrot, cut into strips
1 small green pepper, cored, seeded and
  sliced
125 g (4 oz) baby corn
125 g (4 oz) cauliflower florets
125 g (4 oz) broccoli florets
125 g (4 oz) mangetouts

To make the crêpe batter, sift the flour and salt into a bowl, add the eggs and gradually blend in the milk to form a smooth batter. Stir in the chopped nuts and leave to rest for about 20 minutes.

Heat a crêpe pan and brush with a little oil. Pour in a small amount of batter and swirl to spread thinly and evenly until about 12 cm (5 inches) in diameter. Cook over a moderate heat for 1-2 minutes each side. Remove and keep warm, while cooking the rest of the crêpes.

For the filling, heat the oil in a wok or heavy-based frying pan. Add the garlic, ginger and vegetables, and stir-fry for about 4 minutes until the vegetables are cooked but still crisp.

Divide the filling between the crêpes and roll up. Serve with the duck.

LEMON SHORTCAKE WITH LEMON CREAM AND A LIME COULIS

Shortcake Biscuits:
175 g (6 oz) plain flour
juice of ½ lemon
75 g (3 oz) butter, softened
25 g (1 oz) caster sugar
30 ml (2 tbsp) milk

Lemon Cream:
300 ml (½ pint) whipping cream
finely grated rind and juice of 1 lemon
50 g (2 oz) icing sugar, sifted

Lime Coulis:
juice and finely grated rind of 2 limes
2.5 ml (½ tsp) arrowroot, mixed with a little water
30 ml (2 tbsp) icing sugar
15 ml (1 tbsp) Cointreau

To Decorate:
cocoa powder for dusting
icing sugar, for dusting
strawberries
mint sprigs

To make the shortcake biscuits, sift the flour into a bowl and add the lemon juice, butter, sugar and milk. Mix thoroughly and work to a soft dough, using your hands. Form into a ball, wrap in cling film and leave to rest in the refrigerator for 20 minutes.

Roll out the dough very thinly on a lightly floured surface and cut out 12 biscuits, using a 6 cm (2½ inch) biscuit cutter. Lift onto a baking sheet and bake in a preheated oven at 180°C (350°F) mark 4 for 8-10 minutes, until golden. Leave on the baking sheet for a few minutes, then transfer to a wire rack to cool.

To make the lemon cream, whip the cream in a bowl until soft peaks form, then whisk in the lemon rind and juice with the icing sugar until the mixture thickens. Cover and chill thoroughly in the refrigerator.

To make the lime coulis, put the lime rind and juice in a saucepan and stir in the blended arrowroot and icing sugar. Heat, stirring, until it thickens slightly, just enough to coat the back of the spoon. Allow to cool, then add the Cointreau.

To serve, place a shortcake biscuit in the centre of each serving plate and top with the lemon cream, smoothing it neatly with a palette knife. Dust the tops with cocoa powder and icing sugar. Pour the lime coulis onto the plate to form a pool, and decorate with strawberries and mint sprigs. Serve with the remaining shortbread biscuits.

SEMI-FINAL

MARION MACFARLANE • GARETH RICHARDS • ASHLEY WILSON

PANEL OF JUDGES

Sonia Stevenson • Ken Livingstone • Loyd Grossman

ASHLEY WILSON'S MENU

STARTER

Cheese and Walnut Soufflé

"A lovely dish" **Sonia Stevenson**

MAIN COURSE

Gingered Crab and Sole Layer, with a Rhubarb Sauce

Beetroot with a dash of Balsamic Vinegar

Sesame Potatoes

DESSERT

Chocolate Mille Feuille with Lemon Mousse
and a Caramel Orange Sauce

"I loved the pudding... it was excellent" **Ken Livingstone**

CHEESE AND WALNUT SOUFFLÉ

50 g (2 oz) dry white breadcrumbs
100 ml (3 ½ fl oz) milk
30 g (1 oz) unsalted butter
15 g (½ oz) plain white flour
1 egg yolk
80 g (3¼ oz) mature soft cheese (eg chaumes, maroille, milleens)
3 egg whites
5 ml (1 tsp) lemon juice
75 g (3 oz) walnuts, chopped
salt and freshly ground pepper
60 g (2¼ oz) watercress, trimmed
45 ml (3 tbsp) walnut oil
15 ml (1 tbsp) white wine vinegar

Liberally butter 4 ramekins and coat with a generous layer of breadcrumbs.

Bring the milk to the boil in a small saucepan, then remove from the heat. In another saucepan, melt the butter, stir in the flour and cook for 1-2 minutes. Slowly add the milk, stirring constantly. Bring to the boil and simmer for 1 minute, stirring. Remove from the heat and stir in the egg yolk and soft cheese until smooth.

Whisk the egg whites in a large mixing bowl with a pinch of salt, until soft peaks form. Add the lemon juice and continue whisking until the mixture is smooth and stiff. Beat about a quarter of the egg white into the cheese mixture, then fold in the remainder. Season with salt and pepper.

Half fill the ramekins with the soufflé mixture. Sprinkle 50 g (2 oz) of the chopped walnuts evenly over the surface, then cover with the remaining soufflé.

Stand the ramekins in a bain-marie (roasting tin containing enough water to come halfway up the sides of the dishes). Bake in a preheated oven at 180°C (350°F) mark 4 for 8 minutes. Leave to cool for 10 minutes. Shake the soufflés to loosen them from the ramekins, then turn them out carefully onto a lightly oiled baking sheet. Allow to cool for a further 10 minutes (or longer if more convenient).

Just before serving, return the soufflés to the oven and bake at the same temperature for 5 minutes until the crusts are crisp.

Meanwhile toss the watercress leaves in the walnut oil and wine vinegar and arrange on individual serving plates. Sprinkle with the rest of the chopped walnuts. Serve the hot soufflés on the bed of watercress leaves.

GINGERED CRAB AND SOLE LAYER, WITH A RHUBARB SAUCE

100 g (3½ oz) filo pastry
30 g (1 oz) butter
450 g (1 lb) filleted white fish (eg sole,
*   plaice, cod)*
100 g (3½ oz) young spinach leaves
15 ml (1 tbsp) crème fraîche
2 pieces preserved stem ginger in syrup,
*   finely chopped*
15 ml (1 tbsp) stem ginger syrup
225 g (8 oz) dressed crab meat
salt and freshly ground white pepper
cayenne pepper, to taste

Rhubarb Sauce:
450 g (1 lb) rhubarb
75 g (3 oz) sugar
30 ml (2 tbsp) stem ginger syrup

First make the sauce. Put the rhubarb and sugar in a saucepan with 200 ml (7 fl oz) water. Place over a low heat until the sugar is dissolved, then bring to the boil. Lower the heat and simmer for 10-15 minutes. Strain the sauce through a sieve, pressing through as much juice from the rhubarb as possible. Add the stem ginger syrup and set aside.

Place 3 sheets of filo pastry one on top of another, brushing each sheet with melted butter, then cut out 8 rectangular or diamond shapes, each about 8 x 5 cm (3 x 2 inches). Place on a greased baking sheet and bake in a preheated oven at 200°C (400°F) mark 6 for 5-10 minutes until golden and crisp.

Meanwhile, cut the fish into eight similar-sized pieces. Blanch the spinach in boiling water for 1 minute; drain thoroughly. In a bowl, mix the crème fraîche, ginger and ginger syrup with the crab and season with salt, pepper and cayenne to taste.

Place 4 pieces of fish on a foil-lined baking sheet and cover with half of the spinach. Spoon the crab meat on top, then cover with the remaining spinach. Lay the other fish pieces on top to form 4 neat stacks. Bake in a preheated oven at 200°C (400°F) mark 6 for 10 minutes until the fish is just cooked. Meanwhile reheat the sauce.

Sandwich each 'fish stack' between the cooked filo pastry pieces and serve in a pool of rhubarb sauce, with the accompaniments.

SESAME POTATOES

450 g (1 lb) potatoes (eg Pentland, Desirée,
*   King Edward)*
salt and freshly ground black pepper
15 ml (1 tbsp) sesame oil
1 egg, beaten
45 ml (3 tbsp) sesame seeds

Cook the potatoes in boiling salted water until tender. Drain thoroughly, then mash with the sesame oil. Season with pepper to taste. Allow to cool, then shape into 12 balls, about 2.5 cm (1 inch) in diameter. Dip the balls in the beaten egg, then roll in the sesame seeds to coat.

Bake in a preheated oven at 200°C (400°F) mark 6 for 20 minutes, or until the sesame seeds are golden.

BEETROOT WITH A DASH OF BALSAMIC VINEGAR

2 beetroot
salt and freshly ground black pepper
5 ml (1 tsp) balsamic vinegar

Cook the beetroot in boiling salted water for 30-40 minutes until tender. Drain and allow to cool. Peel the beetroot and cut into small cubes. Reheat before serving. Season with salt and pepper, and toss with the balsamic vinegar.

CHOCOLATE MILLE FEUILLE WITH LEMON MOUSSE AND A CARAMEL ORANGE SAUCE

Chocolate Discs:
160 g (5½ oz) plain couverture chocolate

Mousse:
1 lemon
5 ml (1 tsp) powdered gelatine
2 eggs (size 4)
60 g (2 oz) vanilla caster sugar (see note)
120 ml (4 fl oz) double cream

Sauce:
2 oranges
175 g (6 oz) caster sugar
30 ml (2 tbsp) Grand Marnier or other orange liqueur

To Finish:
icing sugar, for dusting

Draw about 30 circles, 5 cm (2 inches) in diameter, on a sheet of non-stick baking parchment placed on a board or large baking sheet (ie 4 per person plus a few spares in case of breakages).

Melt the chocolate in a bowl over a pan of hot water. Spread the chocolate thinly to cover each circle evenly with the back of a teaspoon, using a circular motion. Leave in a cool place or refrigerate until set.

Using a zester, finely pare the rind from the lemon and one of the oranges. Blanch in boiling water, rinse, then simmer in water to cover for 20 minutes. Drain and allow to cool.

To prepare the mousse, squeeze the juice from the lemon into a small bowl and sprinkle on the gelatine. Leave to soften until spongy. Whisk the egg yolks and sugar in a large bowl until pale and creamy. In a separate bowl, whisk the egg whites until stiff but not dry. Lightly whip the cream in another bowl. Stand the gelatine bowl over a pan of simmering water until dissolved.

Stir the dissolved gelatine into the egg yolk mixture. Continue to stir until the mixture is cool and beginning to thicken; this only takes a few minutes. Fold in the cream, then fold in the whisked egg whites. Refrigerate until set.

To make the sauce, squeeze the juice from the oranges. Melt the sugar in a heavy-based saucepan over a low heat, then increase the heat to moderate and cook, without stirring, until caramelised. Carefully add the orange juice (protecting your hand with a cloth as it will spurt furiously). Heat, stirring until the caramel dissolves. Strain and return to the heat. Add the orange and lemon zest and simmer for 2-3 minutes. Allow to cool, then add the liqueur.

To assemble the dessert, sandwich 4 chocolate discs together with the lemon mousse on each individual serving plate. Dust the tops with icing sugar and pour a pool of sauce around the mille feuilles. Serve at once.

Note: To make your own vanilla sugar, keep a vanilla pod in a jar of caster sugar. It will impart a delicate flavour.

MasterChef 1995
— The Final —
Marion MacFarlane • Clare Askaroff • Holly Schade

Panel of Judges
Raymond Blanc • Rt Hon. William Waldegrave • Loyd Grossman

WINNER

Marion MacFarlane's Menu

Starter
*Skewered Oysters and Scallops
with a Sweet Pepper Sauce*

"I thought the scallops were beautifully cooked, exactly
the right texture" **William Waldegrave**

Main Course
*Saddle of Jacob Lamb with a Black Pudding Stuffing,
served with a Bramble Sauce and Caramelised Apple*

Spinach Purée

Turnip, Potato and Walnut Purée

"Absolutely brilliant" **Raymond Blanc**

Dessert
*Bell Heather Honey and Whisky Ice Cream
with Candied Lemon Shortbread Hearts*

"Incredibly good shortbread" **Loyd**

SKEWERED OYSTERS AND SCALLOPS WITH A SWEET PEPPER SAUCE

8 oysters
8 scallops (4 with corals), cleaned
6 rashers of thin-cut back bacon, preferably
  Ayrshire
2 red peppers
1 yellow pepper
1 orange pepper
10 small shallots, blanched for 2 minutes
  and peeled
5 ml (1 tsp) sugar
75 ml (5 tbsp) Muscadet or other dry white
  wine
8 cloves garlic, peeled
15-30 ml (1-2 tbsp) olive oil
1 onion, thinly sliced
1 thyme sprig, leaves only

To Garnish:
thyme sprigs

Remove the oysters from their shells and carefully roll a piece of bacon round each one. Thread the oysters and scallops alternately onto 4 kebab skewers, allowing 2 oysters and 2 scallops per skewer. Finish each skewer with a scallop coral. Set aside in a cool place until required.

Halve, core and deseed the peppers, then cut each one into 1 cm (½ inch) strips. Cut 8 diamond shapes from the yellow pepper, 8 from the orange pepper, and 16 from the red ones. Set aside.

To make the sauce, chop the remaining red pepper flesh and two of the shallots. Place in a saucepan with 2.5 ml (½ tsp) sugar and the wine. Cook for 10-15 minutes until tender, then work in a food processor or blender until smooth, and pass through a sieve.

Chop the remaining rashers of bacon and fry in a non-stick pan without additional fat until crisp. Remove with a slotted spoon and set aside. Sauté the garlic and the whole shallots in the bacon fat remaining in the pan until golden, adding a little olive oil if needed.

Heat 15 ml (1 tbsp) olive oil in another frying pan, add the sliced onion with the thyme and remaining 2.5 ml (½ tsp) sugar; cook until soft. Add the pepper diamonds and cook until softened. Add the bacon strips and keep warm.

Cook the kebabs under a preheated hot grill for 5-6 minutes, turning once or twice. Meanwhile, reheat the pepper sauce.

To serve, spread a pool of red pepper sauce on each warmed plate. Spoon the onions and pepper diamonds to one side, garnishing with the shallots and garlic. Mark a criss-cross pattern on each scallop with a hot metal skewer and place the kebabs on the sauce. Garnish with thyme and serve at once.

SADDLE OF JACOB LAMB WITH A BLACK PUDDING STUFFING

Jacob lamb is an ancient breed of four-horned sheep. The meat is lean with a superb 'gamey' taste and texture. You could however use traditional Scottish lamb instead. Get your butcher to bone out the saddle for you and remember to ask for the bones which you will need to make a stock.

1 boned saddle of lamb, about 575 g (1¼ lb)

Stuffing:
50 g (2 oz) skinless chicken breast fillet
1 egg
175 g (6 oz) black pudding
1 rosemary sprig, leaves only, finely chopped
salt and freshly ground black pepper

Sauce:
150 ml (¼ pint) blackberry wine, or fruity red wine
300 ml (½ pint) good lamb stock
8 blackberries, squashed
4 peppercorns
5 ml (1 tsp) blackberry jelly
few knobs of butter

Caramelised Apple:
1 Granny Smith apple
25 g (1 oz) unsalted butter
1 large pinch of caster sugar

To Garnish:
16 blackberries

To make the stuffing, process the chicken meat with the egg in a food processor until smooth, then add the black pudding and process until fairly smooth. Add the chopped rosemary and process until evenly mixed.

Spread the stuffing into the boned saddle, roll up and tie at 2.5 cm (1 inch) intervals with cotton string. Keep in a cool place until ready to cook. Place in a roasting tin and cook in a preheated oven at 180°C (350°F) mark 4 for 40 minutes. Remove from the oven, cover loosely with foil and leave to rest in a warm place for 10-15 minutes.

Meanwhile make the sauce. Simmer the blackberry wine until reduced by half. Add the lamb stock and reduce again by half. Add the squashed black-berries and the peppercorns. Leave to infuse for 10 minutes. Add the black-berry jelly and stir until melted. Strain, return to the pan and whisk in the butter to finish the sauce.

To caramelise the apple, peel the apple and cut into wedges. Melt the butter with the sugar in a small frying pan, then add the apple and cook quickly over a high heat until golden brown.

To serve, carve the lamb into 2 cm (¾ inch) slices and arrange on warmed serving plates. Garnish with the caramelised apple and blackberries and carefully spoon the sauce around. Serve at once, with the vegetable purées.

SPINACH PURÉE

450 g (1 lb) young spinach leaves
1 small clove garlic
60 ml (2 fl oz) double cream
knob of butter
freshly grated nutmeg
salt and freshly ground black pepper

Remove the stalks and tough central veins from the spinach, then wash thoroughly. Cook the spinach in a covered pan with just the water clinging to the leaves after washing, and the garlic until just wilted. Drain in a sieve or colander, pressing out excess water.

Transfer to a food processor or blender and chop finely. Add the cream, butter, and nutmeg, salt and pepper to taste. Serve piping hot.

TURNIP, POTATO AND WALNUT PURÉE

350 g (12 oz) turnip, peeled and chopped
125 g (4 oz) potato, peeled and chopped
75 g (3 oz) butter
25 g (1 oz) walnuts, chopped
freshly grated nutmeg
salt and freshly ground black pepper

Cook the turnip and potato in boiling salted water until tender. Drain and purée in a food processor or blender with the butter. Return to the pan and add the walnuts and nutmeg, salt and pepper to taste. Reheat gently to serve if necessary.

BELL HEATHER HONEY AND WHISKY ICE CREAM WITH CANDIED LEMON

I have incorporated all the tastes of the traditional 'hot toddy' in this recipe by using honey, whisky and lemon! The marmalade flavour of the lemon with its slight bitterness counteracts the sweetness of the honey.

Ice Cream:
300 ml (½ pint) double cream
60 ml (4 tbsp) whisky
45-60 ml (3-4 tbsp) bell heather honey
4 egg yolks

Candied Lemon:
1 lemon (unwaxed skin)
125 g (4 oz) caster sugar

To Serve:
Shortbread Hearts (see right)

To make the ice cream, whip the cream until thick, gradually adding the whisky. Heat the honey in a small pan. Meanwhile, whisk the egg yolks in a bowl. Slowly pour the hot honey onto the egg yolks, whisking until the mixture is pale and thick. Fold in the cream. Transfer to a freezerproof container and freeze until firm (see note).

To prepare the candied peel, groove the skin of the lemon lengthwise, using a canelle knife, or sharp knife, then slice thinly, removing the pips. Place the lemon slices in a saucepan, add water to cover and bring to the boil. Simmer for 5 minutes, then drain.

Dissolve the caster sugar in 45 ml (3 tbsp) water in a saucepan, then bring to the boil. Add the lemon slices and simmer gently for 10 minutes until the pith is transparent. Turn into a bowl and leave to cool in the syrup. Cut the candied lemon slices into small segments.

To serve, scoop the ice cream into serving dishes and decorate with a few candied lemon segments. Accompany with the Shortbread Hearts.

Note: An ice-cream maker is not needed because the alcohol content prevents crystals forming during freezing.

SHORTBREAD HEARTS

75 g (3 oz) slightly salted butter
25 g (1 oz) caster sugar
75 g (3 oz) plain flour
25 g (1 oz) fine semolina (farola)
caster sugar, for sprinkling

Cream the butter and sugar together in a bowl. Sift the flour and semolina together onto the creamed mixture and knead in, using your fingertips, until smooth. Press into a greased 18 cm (7 inch) sandwich tin and flatten with a palette knife; it should be about 5 mm (¼ inch) thick. Prick all over with a fork and bake in a preheated oven at 150°C (300°F) mark 2 for 35 minutes. While still warm, cut out shapes, using a heart-shaped cutter. Leave to cool, then sprinkle with caster sugar. Serve two biscuits with each portion of ice cream.

THE FINAL

MARION MACFARLANE • CLARE ASKAROFF • HOLLY SCHADE

PANEL OF JUDGES

Raymond Blanc • Rt Hon. William Waldegrave • Loyd Grossman

CLARE ASKAROFF'S MENU

STARTER

*Warm Smoked Eel Mousses, on a bed of Salad Leaves
with a Lime and Hazelnut Dressing*

"Quite a magical dish, very mellow... perfectly cooked" **Raymond Blanc**

MAIN COURSE

Fillet of Beef with a Herb Crust and Sautéed Mushrooms

Warm Spinach Salad

Sweet Potato Bakes

"The crust on that beef was wonderful, and the sauce was really, really
spectacular" **William Waldegrave**

DESSERT

*Iced Chocolate Puddings, served with
Poached Pears and Caramel Sauce*

"...the pudding – it was really a memorable one" **William Waldegrave**

WARM SMOKED EEL MOUSSES WITH LIME DRESSED SALAD LEAVES

175 g (6 oz) smoked eel, flaked
melted butter, for greasing
250 ml (8 fl oz) double cream
4 egg yolks
15 ml (1 tbsp) chopped chives
2.5 ml (½ tsp) freshly grated nutmeg
pinch of cayenne, to taste
salt and freshly ground black pepper

Salad:
selection of salad leaves and herbs (eg rocket, chicory, radicchio, watercress, frisée, feuille de chêne, flat-leaved parsley, chervil)
4 yellow cherry tomatoes, sliced
few drops of chilli oil

Dressing:
juice of 1 lime
75 ml (5 tbsp) hazelnut oil
10 ml (2 tsp) caster sugar
5 ml (1 tsp) coarse-grain mustard
freshly ground black pepper
rind of 1 lime, removed with a zester

To Garnish:
chervil sprigs

Grease 4 ramekins liberally with melted butter and base-line each with a circle of buttered non-stick baking parchment.

Divide the flaked fish between the ramekins. Mix together the cream, egg yolks, chives, nutmeg and cayenne. Season with plenty of pepper and salt if needed; if the fish is very salty you will only need pepper. Pour the cream mixture over the fish dividing it equally between the dishes; make sure the chives are evenly distributed too. Sprinkle a little cayenne on top.

Place the ramekins on a baking sheet and bake near the top of a preheated oven at 170°C (375°F) mark 3 for 15-20 minutes until well risen and only just firm to the touch.

Meanwhile, prepare the salad, tearing the larger leaves into bite-sized pieces. Arrange the salad leaves and tomatoes in a circle on each serving plate. Drizzle a little chilli oil in between. Shake the ingredients for the dressing together in a screw-topped jar until combined.

Allow the mousses to stand and settle for a few minutes after baking, then turn out and position in the centre of each plate. Garnish with chervil sprigs and drizzle the dressing over the salad. Serve at once, while the mousses are still warm.

Note: After baking, the mousses can be turned out onto a foil-lined baking sheet, then left for several hours if necessary and reheated later. Reheat in the oven, at the above temperature, for 10 minutes.

FILLET OF BEEF WITH A HERB CRUST

Ask your butcher to cut the meat from the middle of the fillet and ensure it is well trimmed to give a neat, even shape.

750 g (1 lb 10 oz) fillet of beef, in one piece
freshly ground black pepper
45 ml (3 tbsp) olive oil
1 egg yolk, beaten

Herb Crust:
4 slices smoked back bacon
25 g (1 oz) pistachio nuts
2 slices granary bread
60 ml (4 tbsp) chopped parsley
50-75 g (2-3 oz) butter, melted
1 clove garlic, crushed
5 ml (1 tsp) coarse-grain mustard
5 ml (1 tsp) Worcestershire sauce
freshly ground black pepper

Sauce:
15 ml (1 tbsp) olive oil
1 onion, chopped
2 large mushrooms, chopped
300 ml (½ pint) brown beef stock
120 ml (4 fl oz) red wine
15 ml (1 tbsp) sherry
salt and freshly ground black pepper

To Serve:
25 g (1 oz) butter
50 g (2 oz) wild mushrooms, or shiitake
squeeze of lemon juice

Begin by making the sauce. Heat the olive oil in a pan, add the onion and mushrooms and cook until golden brown. Pour on the stock and red wine and bring to the boil. Simmer until reduced to a shiny sauce consistency. Strain into a clean pan and add the sherry. Season well. Set aside until ready to serve.

To prepare the herb crust, grill the bacon until crispy; let cool, then chop finely in a food processor. Place in a large shallow dish. Finely chop the nuts in the food processor; add to the bacon. Whizz the bread in the processor to make fine breadcrumbs; add to the dish with the parsley. Mix the melted butter with the garlic, mustard and Worcestershire sauce. Pour onto the crumb mixture, season well with pepper and mix thoroughly. (The bacon will probably add sufficient salt.) Set aside.

Season the meat liberally with pepper. Heat the olive oil in a frying pan and quickly seal the meat on all sides, over a high heat. Cool a little, then brush the top and sides with beaten egg yolk. Coat with the crumb mixture, pressing it very firmly onto the meat to ensure it adheres. Place in a roasting tin and roast in a preheated oven at 190°C (375°F) mark 5 for about 30 minutes to give a rare meat.

Shortly before serving, reheat the sauce. Heat the butter in another pan and sauté the mushrooms until they have just softened. Add a squeeze of lemon juice and pepper to taste.

Leave the beef to rest for a few minutes after cooking, then carve into thick slices, allowing 2-3 per person. Arrange on warmed serving plates with the wild mushrooms. Pour on the sauce and serve accompanied by the warm spinach salad and sweet potato bakes.

SWEET POTATO BAKES

Use the orange-fleshed variety of sweet potato for this dish.

675 g (1½ lb) sweet potatoes
salt and freshly ground black pepper
40-50 g (1½-2 oz) butter
grated rind of 1 orange, plus a little juice if necessary
seeds from 4 cardamom pods, freshly ground
15 ml (1 tbsp) light muscovado sugar

Peel the sweet potatoes and cut into cubes. Cook in boiling salted water for about 10 minutes until soft. Drain thoroughly.

Mash the potatoes with the butter, then stir in the orange rind (see note). Season liberally with salt and pepper. Divide the mixture between four buttered ramekins.

Mix the ground cardamom seeds with the brown sugar and sprinkle on top of each ramekin. Top with a small knob of butter. Pop under a preheated grill until the sugar has caramelised. Alternatively place in a preheated oven at 180°C (350°F) mark 4 for 10 minutes.

Note: If the mixture seems at all dry, stir in a little of the juice from the orange.

WARM SPINACH SALAD

350 g (12 oz) spinach leaves
25 g (1 oz) sun-dried tomatoes in oil,
   drained and roughly chopped
25 g (1 oz) pecan nuts, roughly chopped
1 clove garlic, crushed
2 spring onions, sliced
15 g (½ oz) freshly grated Parmesan cheese
30 ml (2 tbsp) oil from the sun-dried
   tomatoes
black pepper

To Garnish:
2 parsnips
few flat-leaved parsley sprigs
groundnut oil, for deep-frying
coarse sea salt

To prepare the garnish, peel the parsnips and pare long thin shreds, using a zester. Mix with a few sprigs of flat-leaved parsley. Heat the oil for deep-frying, then deep-fry the parsnip shreds and parsley, in batches, for about 1 minute until crispy. Remove with a slotted spoon and drain on kitchen paper. Immediately season with freshly ground salt; keep warm.

Meanwhile, steam the spinach for about 4 minutes until just wilted, then chop roughly. Place in a bowl with the rest of the ingredients and mix well. Served while still warm, or at room temperature; do not refrigerate. Pile the deep-fried parsnips and parsley on top of the salad to serve.

POACHED PEARS

4 dessert pears, ripe but firm (preferably
   Rocha)
600 ml (1 pint) white wine
150 g (5 oz) caster sugar
5 ml (1 tsp) allspice
2 finely pared strips of lemon zest, each
   about 5 x 1 cm (2 x ½ inch)

Put the wine, sugar, allspice and lemon zest into a large pan. Heat gently until the sugar has dissolved, then simmer gently.

Meanwhile, carefully peel each pear, leaving the stalk intact. Halve lengthwise leaving the stalk attached to one half. Scoop out the core. Immediately immerse in a bowl of cold water with the lemon juice added to prevent discolouration.

Place the pear halves, cut-side down, in the simmering wine syrup. Return to the boil, cover and simmer gently for 10-15 minutes until tender.

Remove from the heat and leave the pears to cool in the cooking liquid a little, then lift out and drain on kitchen paper. Set aside until ready to serve.

To serve, slice the pear halves with stalks lengthwise, leaving the stalk end intact, and fan out. Use the other pear halves for the chocolate pudding filling (see page 168).

ICED CHOCOLATE PUDDINGS

75 g (3 oz) good quality dark chocolate
15 ml (1 tbsp) cooled strong black coffee
  (5 ml/1 tsp instant coffee dissolved in a
  little water)
2 eggs, separated
150 ml (¼ pint) double cream
pinch of salt

Filling:
4 poached pear halves (see right)
150 ml (¼ pint) double cream
4 amaretti biscuits, crushed
30 ml (2 tbsp) amaretto di Saronno liqueur

Caramel Sauce:
50 g (2 oz) caster sugar
120-150 ml (4-5 fl oz) double cream
15 ml (1 tbsp) amaretto di Saronno liqueur

To Serve:
cocoa powder, for dusting
Poached Pears (see page 167)

Break the chocolate into pieces and place in a heatproof bowl with the coffee. Place over a pan of boiling water, until melted; stir until smooth. Remove from the heat and beat in the egg yolks, one at a time. In a separate bowl, whip the cream until thick.

In another bowl, whisk the egg whites with a pinch of salt until very stiff. Fold the whipped cream into the chocolate mixture, then fold in the egg whites. Transfer to an ice-cream maker and churn for 10-15 minutes. (Alternatively freeze in a suitable container until firm, but not solid.)

Meanwhile, line 4 individual pudding basins or ramekins with cling film and place in the freezer to chill. When the ice cream has become quite stiff, spoon into the lined basins, spreading it evenly up the sides of the basins and leaving a hollow in the centre.

Stand the basins on a plate or small tray and freeze for about 2 hours. Check after 15 minutes or so, that the ice cream has not softened and slipped down the sides of the basins; if necessary re-shape at this stage and return to the freezer.

To make the caramel sauce, dissolve the sugar in 30 ml (2 tbsp) water in a heavy-based pan over a low heat. Bring to the boil and cook to a rich golden caramel. Take off the heat and let cool slightly until the bubbles subside. Carefully add the cream, stirring.

Return to the heat and reheat gently, stirring, until all the caramel has dissolved. (If a few lumps refuse to dissolve, strain into a bowl.) Leave the sauce to cool, then stir in the liqueur, and a little more cream if the sauce thickens too much on cooling.

Shortly before serving, prepare the filling for the puddings. Cut the poached pear halves into small chunks. Whip the cream until thick, then fold in the chopped pears, crushed amaretti biscuits and liqueur.

Remove the chocolate puddings from the freezer and fill the centres with the creamy pear mixture. Dust one half of each serving plate with sifted cocoa. Unmould the puddings and position on the plates. Pour a small pool of caramel sauce alongside and arrange the fanned pear halves on top. Serve at once.

THE FINAL

MARION MACFARLANE • CLARE ASKAROFF • HOLLY SCHADE

PANEL OF JUDGES

Raymond Blanc • Rt Hon. William Waldegrave • Loyd Grossman

HOLLY SCHADE'S MENU

STARTER

*Ravioli of Mascarpone and Boursin Cheese
with Fennel and Pine Nut Butter*

"The pasta was very nice and thin" **Raymond Blanc**

MAIN COURSE

Braised Lamb Shanks

Colcannon

Minted Carrots

"...a typical lovely wholesome dish... very nicely done" **Raymond Blanc**

DESSERT

*Chocolate Gelato with Bitter Orange Sauce,
served in Chocolate Cups*

"The chocolate ice cream was very good" **Raymond Blanc**

RAVIOLI OF RICOTTA AND BOURSIN CHEESE WITH FENNEL AND PINE NUT BUTTER

To make the ravioli dough, you will need a pasta machine. For optimum results, use Italian '00' pasta flour. If unobtainable substitute plain flour.

Pasta Dough:
310 g (10½ oz) '00' flour
2.5 ml (½ tsp) salt
3 eggs (size 2)
25 ml (1 fl oz) olive oil (approximately)

Filling:
2 cloves garlic, crushed
15 ml (1 tbsp) olive oil
225 g (8 oz) ricotta cheese
175 g (6 oz) Boursin cheese
1 egg (size 2)
30 ml (2 tbsp) finely chopped basil

Topping:
75 g (3 oz) butter
60 ml (4 tbsp) olive oil
1 fennel bulb, cored and finely chopped
50 g (2 oz) pine nuts
3 ripe plum tomatoes, seeded and chopped
30 ml (2 tbsp) finely chopped basil
25 g (1 oz) Parmesan cheese, freshly grated

To Garnish:
basil leaves

To make the ravioli dough, put the flour, salt, eggs and olive oil in a food processor and process about 30 seconds until a smooth dough is formed. If necessary, add a little more olive oil to help the dough come together. Wrap in cling film and flatten. Leave to rest in the refrigerator for 30 minutes.

To make the ravioli filling, sauté the garlic in the olive oil until softened, then transfer to a bowl. Add all of the remaining ingredients and whisk with an electric beater until smooth.

Cut off about one quarter of the ravioli dough and re-wrap the remainder. Flatten the piece of dough slightly and dust with flour. Pass through the pasta machine on its widest setting, then fold the dough and pass through the machine repeatedly, narrowing the setting by one notch each time until you each the last but one setting. Dust lightly with flour, cover with a tea-towel and set aside. Repeat with the rest of the dough.

Using a 7.5 cm (3 inch) pastry cutter cut 30 circles from the pasta dough. Place a rounded teaspoon of the filling in the centre of 15 circles. Moisten the edges of the other 15 circles and place over the filling. Press the edges together to seal. Leave the ravioli on a tea-towel and allow to dry slightly before cooking.

Meanwhile, prepare the topping. Heat the butter and 45 ml (3 tbsp) olive oil in a pan, add the fennel and sauté for 3 minutes or until soft; keep warm. Heat the remaining 15 ml (1 tbsp) olive oil in a frying pan and toast the pine nuts until browned. Warm the tomatoes through in a pan.

Cook the ravioli in a large pan of boiling water for 4-5 minutes until *al dente* (tender but firm to the bite). Drain and arrange on warmed serving plates. Top with the buttered fennel, pine nuts, chopped tomatoes and basil. Sprinkle the Parmesan on top and garnish with basil leaves. Serve immediately.

BRAISED LAMB SHANKS

8 small lamb shanks or 4 medium ones
45 ml (3 tbsp) olive oil
1 onion, chopped
4 cloves garlic, crushed
50 g (2 oz) tomato purée
2 carrots, sliced
125 g (4 oz) canned chopped tomatoes
350 ml (12 fl oz) red wine
350 ml (12 fl oz) lamb stock
5 ml (1 tsp) finely chopped rosemary leaves
5 ml (1 tsp) finely chopped thyme leaves
2.5 ml (½ tsp) allspice
salt and freshly ground black pepper
5-10 ml (1-2 tsp) arrowroot, mixed with a
  little water
thyme sprigs, to garnish

Heat half of the olive oil in a heavy flameproof casserole. Add the onion and sauté for 3-4 minutes until soft. Add the garlic and cook for a further 2 minutes. Add the tomato purée, carrots, tomatoes, wine, stock, herbs, allspice and seasoning. Bring to the boil.

Meanwhile, heat the remaining olive oil in a heavy-based frying pan and brown the lamb shanks on all sides. Add the lamb to the casserole, cover and cook in a preheated oven at 180°C (350°F) mark 4 for 1½-2 hours, stirring from time to time, until the meat comes away from the bone easily. Lower the oven temperature to 110°C (225°F) mark ¼.

Lift the lamb shanks out of the casserole and place in an ovenproof dish; keep warm in the oven. Strain the sauce into a saucepan and boil steadily until reduced by about half. Add the arrowroot to thicken the sauce slightly if necessary, and heat, stirring, until thickened.

Place the lamb shanks on warmed serving plates and pour over the sauce. Garnish with thyme and serve with minted carrots and the colcannon.

COLCANNON

6 medium potatoes
1 green cabbage, cored and chopped
185 ml (6 fl oz) double cream
75 g (3 oz) butter
2 cloves garlic, crushed
salt and freshly ground black pepper

Peel and quarter the potatoes, then cook in boiling salted water until tender. Drain well and mash with the cream, using a potato ricer or masher.

Meanwhile, steam the cabbage for 5 minutes. Heat the butter in a large heavy-based saucepan and sauté the garlic for about 2 minutes until softened. Add the cabbage and cook for about 5 minutes until soft.

Purée the cabbage in a food processor, then mix with the creamed potato and mash well. Season with salt and pepper to taste. Serve piping hot.

CHOCOLATE GELATO WITH BITTER ORANGE SAUCE, IN CHOCOLATE CUPS

Ice Cream:
225 g (8 oz) sugar
500 ml (16 fl oz) milk
125 g (4 oz) cocoa powder, sifted
100 g (3½ oz) plain dark chocolate
4 large egg yolks

Chocolate Cups:
175 g (6 oz) dark chocolate, in pieces

Orange Sauce:
30 ml (2 tbsp) caster sugar
30 ml (2 tbsp) finely pared orange zest,
  shredded
250 ml (8 fl oz) freshly squeezed orange juice
125 g (4 oz) orange marmalade
15 ml (1 tbsp) Grand Marnier or other
  orange liqueur

To make the ice cream, melt 50 g (2 oz) of the sugar in a large heavy-based saucepan over a low heat, without stirring. Increase the heat to moderate and cook, stirring with a fork, until it forms a deep golden brown caramel. Remove from the heat and briefly dip the base of the pan into a bowl of iced water to stop further cooking; the caramel will harden at this stage. Leave to cool for 5 minutes, then add the milk and return to the heat, whisking until the caramel has melted. Whisk in the cocoa until well combined; keep warm.

Meanwhile, melt the chocolate in a heatproof bowl over a pan of simmering water or in the microwave on MEDIUM.

In another bowl, beat the egg yolks and remaining 175 g (6 oz) sugar, together until thick and pale. Gradually whisk in the caramel mixture, then the melted chocolate until evenly combined. Transfer to a clean saucepan and cook gently until the custard thickens slightly, just enough to lightly coat the back of a wooden spoon. Pour into a bowl set over another bowl of iced water to cool. Freeze in an ice-cream maker. (If you don't have an ice-cream machine, freeze in a suitable container, whisking 2-3 times during freezing.)

To prepare the chocolate cups, melt the chocolate in a heatproof bowl over a pan of simmering water or in the microwave on MEDIUM. Stir until smooth, then allow to cool until it begins to thicken again. Take a teaspoonful of the melted chocolate and drizzle around the top inside edge of a paper muffin case, allowing it to drip down the sides and line the base. Spread the chocolate to coat the sides and base of the paper case evenly, adding a little more if necessary. Do not use too much chocolate, only 5-10 ml (1-2 tsp) per paper cup. Repeat to make 6 or 8 cups (see note). As the chocolate cools, it may drip down the sides to the base; if so spread it back up the sides, otherwise the base of the cups will be too thick. Chill until firm.

To make the sauce, melt the sugar in a MEDIUM heavy-based pan over a low heat, without stirring. Increase the heat to moderate and cook, stirring with a fork, until it forms a golden caramel. Remove from the heat and allow to cool.

While the caramel is cooking, blanch the orange zest in a small pan of boiling water for 15 seconds; drain.

Add the orange zest and juice to the caramel. Cook over a moderate heat, stirring until the caramel is melted. Whisk in the marmalade until evenly combined. Stir in the Grand Marnier and remove from the heat. Allow to cool.

Fill 4 chocolate cups with the ice cream and freeze until the ice cream is firm. Peel away the paper cases and place on individual serving plates. Surround with the sauce and serve at once.

Note: Make a few extra chocolate cups, to allow for breakages.

INDEX

OF RECIPE TITLES AND CONTESTANTS